DEDICATED TO

Bernard G. Berenson, Ph.D.,
my life-long friend and interdependent
processor who has devoted his life to
human capital development.

Human Possibilities—

Human Capital
in the 21st Century

by

Robert R. Carkhuff, Ph.D.

Copyright © 2000, Robert R. Carkhuff

Published by: Possibilities Publishing
22 Amherst Road
Amherst, MA 01002
800-822-2801 (U.S. and Canada)
413-253-3488
413-253-3490 (fax)
www.possibilitiespublisher.com

Editorial services by Robie Grant
Production services by Jean Miller
Cover design by Eileen Klockars

HUMAN POSSIBILITIES—
HUMAN CAPITAL IN THE 21ˢᵀ CENTURY

Contents

ABOUT THE AUTHOR vii
PREFACE ix
FOREWORD—David N. Aspy xiii

I. INTRODUCTION AND OVERVIEW 1
   1. The Evolution of HCD 3
      • Dependency 5
      • Independency 9
      • Interdependency 13
   2. The Ingredients of HCD 19
      The Areas and Dimensions of HCD 25
      Levels of HCD 29

II. THE HCD INGREDIENTS 39
   3. Physical Fitness—The Energizers 41
   4. Personal Motivation—The Catalyzers 65
   5. Interpersonal Relating—The Facilitators 89
   6. Information Relating—The Operationalizers 113
   7. Information Representing—The Modelers 137
   8. Individual Processing—The Thinkers 161
   9. Interpersonal Processing—The Shared Processors 191
  10. Interdependent Processing—The Actualizers 217

III. SUMMARY AND TRANSITION 241
  11. The HCD Operations 243
  12. The HCD Equation 253

APPENDICES 263
    The Evolution of HCD Systems 265
    Bibliography 273
    Acknowledgments 281

ABOUT THE AUTHOR

ROBERT R. CARKHUFF, PH.D.

- One of the most-cited social scientists of our time and author of three of the most-referenced books in the 20th century

- Founder and Chairman of Human Technology, Inc., Carkhuff Thinking Systems, Inc., and Carkhuff Institute of Human Technology

- Visionary of *The Possibilities Economics* and *The Possibilities Culture*

- Generator of *The New Science of Possibilities*

PREFACE

Human Possibilities

The Cassandrans have been predicting the demise of American workers for generations. According to their predictions, the Soviet Union should now reign supreme because of the excellence of their training in math and science. According to their predictions, Japan should have long since taken over technological leadership because of the failure of our educational systems.

Guess what? Less than 15 percent of our workforce is going to require skills in math and science. Know what else? Nearly two-thirds (and growing) of our workers are going to require thinking skills: the ability to generate new and more productive ways of doing things.

This quandary reminds me of what they used to say about the old Washington Senators baseball team:

> *"Washington—first in war, first in peace, and last in the American League."*

It seems to me that the critics are forced to say something similar:

> *"Washington—last in science, last in math, and first in the Global Economic League!"*

Now we must be doing something right, mustn't we? Here is what we are doing right:

- We have a culture oriented towards future requirements rather than past traditions.

- We have a capitalistic economic system disposed to entrepreneurial-driven, free enterprise rather than command-and-control economics.

- We have a free democratic governance system increasingly oriented electronically toward direct democracy rather than authoritarian and totalitarian governance.

What does this mean for the workforce in the 21st century?

- We have a virtual monopoly on the generators of technological breakthroughs. This means that we have the most powerful generative thinkers in the history of the world.

- We have legions of innovators who can take these breakthroughs and transfer them to a myriad of areas.

- We have armies of commercializers who can apply these transfers to spiraling arrays of products and services.

What kinds of skills, knowledge and attitudes must "Workforce XXI" have to become generators, innovators and commercializers? That is the thesis of this book, **Human Possibilities.** That is the mission of Human Capital Development.

First of all, it is thinking systems that make humans *"capital"* or most important. Above all else, these thinking systems emphasize interdependent processing systems: the capacity to become *"one"* with any phenomena—product or service, task or mission—in order to engage in *"mutual processing for mutual benefit."* Interdependent processing systems are the overriding requirement of the 21st century global marketplace and workplace. Interdependent processing skills are the most powerful contributors to individual performance, unit production, organizational productivity, corporate profitability, extended enterprise market share and marketplace growth.

In support of these prepotent interdependent processing systems are the following:

- Interpersonal processing skills that systematically negotiate merged and improved images of any phenomena;

- Individual processing skills that systematically generate entirely new and productive images of the phenomena;

- Information representing systems that produce multidimensional images of phenomena to empower processing;

- Information relating systems that yield operational images of data and conceptual information to enable information representation.

Preconditions for these intellectual processing skills are the emotional and physical support systems:

- Interpersonal relating systems that enable us to relate to the people, data and things in our worlds;

- Motivational systems that inspire us to achieve the highest standards for the people, data and things in our worlds;

- Fitness systems that energize the other emotional and intellectual systems.

Together, these physical, emotional and intellectual resource systems define the requirements for the 21st century workplace:

- Physical skills that *energize* processing;

- Emotional skills that *catalyze* processing;

- Intellectual skills that *actualize* processing.

These are the systems that operationally define *"Human Possibilities"*:

> *Intellectual processing deliveries discharged by emotional support systems enabled by physical preconditions.*

These are the systems that will define yet another century of leadership in a global marketplace characterized by interdependent relating, free enterprise economics and direct democratic governance.

These are the productive ingredients of Human Capital Development.

RRC

McLean, Virginia
January, 2000

FOREWORD
HCD—The Human Mission
by David N. Aspy, Ed.D.

It is no accident that Carkhuff and his associates have culminated a lifetime of effort in defining the skills of human capital development, or HCD. Indeed, Carkhuff provides the only operational definition of the skills, knowledge and attitudes required for HCD or, more simply, growth. Carkhuff defines HCD precisely as *"interdependent processing"* and its necessary physical fitness, motivation, interpersonal relating, information relating and representing, and human processing skills—individual, interpersonal and interdependent.

In the 1960s, summarized in his classic two volumes on *Helping and Human Relations,* Carkhuff developed a comprehensive model of emotional and intellectual development that presented demonstrable elements that could be learned and used in all learning contexts. In our own work in education, we were privileged to produce the most extensive research ever conducted supporting the contributions of Carkhuff's emotional and intellectual skills to learning outcomes in a variety of educational settings.[1]

In the 1970s, Carkhuff summarized the dramatic results of the most comprehensive community-based human resource development programs ever conducted in his path-finding book on *The Development of Human Resources.* Working with Drs. B.G. Berenson and A.H. Griffin, Carkhuff empowered underemployed and disenfranchised citizens with the living, learning and working skills to define their own destinies and resurrect an entire community. In so doing, Carkhuff contributed the first comprehensive models of learning, and so, training and development. Succinctly, he and his colleagues concluded that *we are what we are empowered to be.* Carkhuff has gone on to expand upon these empowering strategies in all of his ongoing Human Capital Development efforts.

In the 1980s, Carkhuff summarized the results of his extensive private and public sector HRD demonstrations in his revolutionary text on *Toward Actualizing Human Potential.* The basic contribution of these projects was the elaboration of the processing systems: exploring by analyzing experience; understanding by synthesizing goals; acting by operationalizing programs. This was the first articulation of a systematic human thinking or generating system. This threshold discovery enables human beings not only to control their own

---

[1] Aspy, D.N., and Roebuck, F.N. *Kids Don't Learn From People They Don't Like.* Amherst, MA: HRD Press, 1977.

destinies but, moreover, to free their own destinies, to actualize the potentially infinite power of their brains, to actualize their humanity!

While Carkhuff and his associates were concerned primarily with the individual development, or ID track, of HRD, they were not oblivious to the simultaneous and parallel development of the organizational development, or OD, track. Indeed, Carkhuff was dedicated to the convergence of these two seemingly disparate tracks: the one, the ID track, committed to empowering individuals from their internal frames of reference; the other, the OD track, dedicated to selecting and training individuals to serve larger organizational functions. In the 1980s, Carkhuff developed the first systematic models for operationalizing and integrating organizational productivity (*The Sources of Human Productivity*) and individual performance (*The Exemplar*).

Basically, these models indicated that we cannot have one without the other: individual performance without organizational productivity, and vice versa.

Carkhuff elaborated upon the implications of this principle of interdependency by introducing *The Age of the New Capitalism,* a vision that diminished the contributions of the old financial capital ingredients and accentuated the contributions of the New Capital ingredients of human, information and organizational capital. We now live in *"The Age of the New Capitalism!"* The degree to which we address and process these New Capital ingredients will guide our socioeconomic destinies. In this context, Carkhuff has contributed a pathfinding text, *Empowering,* to guide all of us into leadership roles in the 21st century.

In the 1990s, it remained for Carkhuff and his associates to fully integrate the ID and the OD tracks. They have done this in two books introducing the 21st century: *The Possibilities Leader,* which emphasizes the ID track, and *The Possibilities Organization,* which emphasizes the OD track. Together, they define *"The Possibilities Management System."* This is the first real management system ever! Everything else has been one form or another of the old military hierarchical system.

Now in this volume, *Human Possibilities,* Carkhuff introduces the reader to the HCD skills required by the 21st century marketplace. This is the first model in human history to operationally define human capital development. This volume which you are about to read introduces us to the conditions and preconditions of human capital development. The central message is that the power in HCD lies in intellectual processing, and that intellectual processing culminates in interdependent processing. Carkhuff presents the intellectual preconditions of interdependent processing: individual and interpersonal processing. The preconditions of intellectual processing are informational relating and representing. In turn, the preconditions of these processing dimensions are emotional dimensions: the motivation to engage people or phenomena, and the interpersonal skills to relate to people or phenomena. Finally, the precondition of the emotional and intellectual dimensions is the physical dimension: the fitness to provide the energy to relate and process. This is the substance of human growth and development. It prepares us for actualizing our brainpower and, therefore, our human potential. It prepares us for meeting the interdependent processing requirements of the global marketplace in the 21st century.

This review would not be complete if the reviewer did not point out Carkhuff's unique contributions to the future of civilization. Carkhuff is widely recognized as the first creator of systematic interpersonal communication systems. Perhaps not so widely recognized was his development and demonstration of the first operational learning and thinking systems and, relatedly, human resource development models. All of these individual processing systems are presented here. All of them are milestones in the evolution of humanity.

Perhaps Carkhuff and Berenson and their colleagues have made their greatest contribution to science in their *New Science of Possibilities*. In these volumes, they define the new processing science and its derivative technologies. They view the new possibilities science and its *"paradigmatic"* technologies as driving the old probabilities science and its parametric technologies.

However, Carkhuff's most lasting contribution to the march of civilization is interdependent processing. It is inevitable, according to Carkhuff, that we relate interdependently in order to survive and grow in the 21st century. In addition to delivering a vision of global interdependency, Carkhuff does what no one else has even dared: he is the first human being on the face of the Earth to operationalize interdependency with observable, measurable and repeatable skills! If we can grasp the fundamental truth and value of interdependency and implement the human technologies that Carkhuff has given us, then we can, indeed, fulfill our human destiny!

DNA   Edmonds, Oklahoma
University of Oklahoma   January, 2000

$$HCD = P \bullet E^2 \bullet I^5$$

I

Introduction and Overview

1. The Evolution of HCD

DEPENDENCY

Perhaps the most distinguishing characteristic of the Industrial Age was that people were asked to act—and not to think! Indeed, they were considered as *"labor"* and defined in terms of *"physical exertion."* People were simply handed *"unthinking tasks"* to perform. They were prepared by being conditioned or reinforced to make the appropriate reflex responses. For example, in manufacturing, they might have stamped a product over and over; in sales, they may have manipulated customers to buy a product; in distribution, they might have filled an order in a prescribed way. In the paradigm of human processing, someone higher in the hierarchy explored the data, understood the goals, and then *"handed-off"* action tasks to totally dependent performers. In the ultimate test of dependency, there would be no performance without that *"hand-off."*

Dependency—Acting without Thinking

To be sure, it was in these performers' self-interest to be dependent. After all, they were viewed as mere mechanical appendages to the industrial machinery, inexpensive and replaceable parts as it were. They were *"shaped"* by differential reinforcements which punished lethargy and rewarded energy. They functioned in authoritarian settings, driven by *"top-down"* dictations. They dedicated themselves only to keeping life orderly, to thinking within the lines drawn for them, to being obedient to the corporate source of their livelihood. Above all else, there was no processing! No exploring of human experience! No understanding of human goals! Just unthinking action!

Industrial Age Conditions

In its simplest form, conditioned behavior is viewed in terms of a *stimulus* → *response* or $S \rightarrow R$ sequence. There is no intervention between stimulus and response. When the stimulus is presented, the response is emitted, similar to the way a knee muscle reflexes to a tap. While there are sets of anticipatory s–r responses, there is no intelligence or intentionality mediating the sequence or relationship of stimulus and response. The conditioned responder simply reacts in an unthinking or mechanical manner. Reduced, the *"condition"*—or stimulus complex—determines the person's response. Thus, the cultural or *"conditioning"* context determines the individual's behavior. The conditioned performer is a dependent person.

S → R Conditioning

While conditioned responding may be appropriate under specified and unchanging conditions, it becomes increasingly inappropriate with changing conditions. The dependent person's response to *"diminished returns"* from unchanging investments is to *"work harder."* Spiraling changes in conditions condemn conditioned response training efforts to failure. Indeed, over time and with changes, conditioned responding becomes increasingly pathological. These responses simply do not relate to the stimuli to which they were conditioned. Or, put another way, the responses become *"functionally autonomous"* or *"autistic."* Fortunately, the *"working harder"* response to crises is ultimately sentenced to extinction by the punishment schedule of reinforcements: delivering increasing *"shocks"* to the human system to match increasing exertions of conditioned human effort.

"Working Harder"

Independency

The movement from dependency to independency was a significant social step. People were now involved in the understanding process preceding action. As the authorities or bosses became more and more burdened by data input, they began to share some of the responsibility of processing. The authorities still explored the data. They retained control of understanding the strategic goals. They did, however, hand off the goals. Accordingly, the performers participated in decision-making and problem-solving activities. They became involved in designing the systems to achieve the goals. They took responsibility for the implementation of the systems. In order to do this, the performers needed to expand their repertoire of responses to manage their new responsibilities.

Independency—Acting with Understanding

To be sure, it was in the best interest of the performers to be independent. Whereas Industrial Age labor was valued for its dependency, Data Age *"human resources"* were valued for their independent contribution. These independent performers were differentiated by their accumulated repertoires of responses. They related laterally as well as vertically in participative settings to share *"known"* responses. They participated in *"quality circles," "teambuilding," "participative management," "consensus-building."* As opposed to corporate obedience, these performers were characterized by corporate identification: they simply identified their welfare with the welfare of the corporation. Above all else, they shared in the understanding of the goals before acting upon the programs.

Data Age Conditions

Processing in the Data Age was based upon the sharing of conditioned responses. The Data Age defined its requirements in terms of *"participative learning."* The difference between *participative learning* and conditioned responding is the intervening human organism (O) which discriminates the stimulus (S), intervenes to mediate by selecting an appropriate response, and emits the response (R). Of course, in order to make appropriate responses, it is assumed that the organism has a repertoire of conditioned or S–R responses. In other words, the individual acquires a set of responses from which to draw. Depending upon the stimuli, the individual simply discriminates the stimuli and formulates an appropriate response. The performer's independence is found in the completeness of his or her response repertoire. The limitations are found in the fact that the repertoire is comprised entirely of conditioned responses.

S–O–R Learning

I. Introduction and Overview

"Participative learning" serves to increase the response repertoire and enable the performer to *"work smarter."* *Working smarter* simply means that the performer collects and selects from among the available *"best practices"* for performing a task productively. The problem is that task requirements today are changing so rapidly that we quickly exhaust the *"known responses."* While the sharing and building of known responses may serve to extend their utility, sooner, rather than later, our escalating *"meetings"* reach the point of *"diminishing returns."* In times of rapid change we simply cannot meet enough to develop a *"consensus response."* And, the *working smarter* approach *"runs out of gas"* when completely new and innovative responses are required by the changing marketplace.

"Working Smarter"

Interdependency

If it was a large step from dependency to independency, then it is a gigantic step forward to interdependency. As authorities or bosses are overwhelmed by *"information overload,"* they begin to share the responsibility for total processing. They *"hand off"* the entire data base for processing. They cede responsibility for exploring experiences, understanding the goals, and acting upon the programs. Accordingly, the performers conduct all of the processing activities. In order to do so, the performers, plainly and simply, have to learn a whole new set of processing skills. Moreover, they have to learn to process interdependently.

Interdependency—Exploring, Understanding, Acting

To be sure, it is in the best interest of the performers to be interdependent. *"Human capital"* or thinking humans are now increasingly viewed as the generative *"source of effect."* In turn, information modeling is viewed as a *"synergistic partner."* These interdependent processors are driven by shared missions. They exist in highly interactive *"thinking environments."* They are required to process highly complex and curvilinear, multidimensional phenomena into useful models, systems, objectives, programs and tasks. Beyond corporate identification, they emphasize entrepreneurial and intrapreneurial initiative based upon their processing orientation. Above all else, they conduct the entire process, thinking individually before processing interpersonally and interdependently—for team, unit, organization, marketplace, community, region, nation, alliance and global purposes.

Information Age Conditions

Processing in the Information Age is based upon the need for the continuous generation of new and more productive responses. The Information Age defines its requirements as *"generative thinking."* The difference between participative learning and generative thinking is the difference between *"best practices"* and best processes for creating new and better responses; or, put another way, between quantitative responses and qualitative responses. In generative thinking, an active and generative human processor (P) intervenes between the stimulus (S) and the response (R). At the extreme, a skilled human processor has the potential to create responses that the stimulus materials were never conditioned to elicit.

S–P–R Thinking

Generative thinking is the process of generating responses or *"thinking better." Thinking better* simply means that the performer is able to generate new and more productive ways of doing things under all circumstances. A person who is *thinking better* assumes that all of our *"current operating procedures"* are inadequate and so generates *"productive operating procedures"* to create whole new ways of doing things. Even when we have generated new principles individually, we go on to process interdependently with our partners. This way, we can generate still more productive responses than we, as individuals, are able to generate.

"Thinking Better"

Interdependency is the theme of this book. Indeed, interdependent processing and the growth it leads to defines the human capital development, or HCD, process. Interdependency is a new and demanding requirement. It asks that we set aside our reactions to dependency and our fetish for independency. It demands a commitment to co-mingle our *"processing blood"* with that of others for our mutual benefit. It requires an intimacy with information at the level of a love relationship. Above all else, it requires a suspension of our independent motives in the interest of mutual benefits. In short, it asks that we elevate our values and dedicate our systematic processing for our growing *"human family."*

Interdependent Growth

2. The Ingredients of HCD

The purpose of life is to grow. All manner of life grows physically—in size and sinew and muscle. Humans are unique in that they also grow in many other ways. They grow emotionally—in their motivation to accomplish things in their own lives—and interpersonally—in their relationships to the emotions and motivations of others. They grow intellectually—in their abilities to process information inputs into results outputs. We may say that human growth is human capital development (HCD).

Human Growth = HCD

Human Growth Is HCD

Indeed, we may say that human growth or human capital development is physical, emotional and intellectual development. At another level, we may view the multiplying effects of each dimension upon the other. Our physical energy level multiplies the effects of our emotional make-up; our emotions multiply the effects of our intellectual processing. In turn, the intellectual dimension contributes the *"pull"* of intellectual pursuits to energize and motivate human performance.

$$HCD = P \bullet E \bullet I$$

HCD Is a Function of P • E • I

In analyzing the dimensions of human growth and development, we may employ the outline of the Human Capital Development model found in Table 1. Here we find the areas and dimensions of HCD as well as the levels of functioning on these dimensions. The physical area emphasizes fitness. The emotional area emphasizes motivation and interpersonal relating. The intellectual area emphasizes informational relating and representing and all forms of processing: individual, interpersonal, interdependent. The levels of functioning include the following: leaders, contributors, participants, observers and detractors. We will fill in this outline with our learnings concerning the different dimensions of HCD.

The HCD Model

I. Introduction and Overview

Table 1. HUMAN CAPITAL DEVELOPMENT

LEVELS OF FUNCTIONING	PHYSICAL	EMOTIONAL		INTELLECTUAL				
	Physical Fitness	Personal Motivation	Interpersonal Relating	Information Relating	Information Representing	Individual Processing	Interpersonal Processing	Inter-dependent Processing
Leader								
Contributor								
Participant								
Observer								
Detractor								

The Areas and Dimensions of HCD

The areas emphasize the physical, emotional and intellectual factors that lead to human growth and development:

- Physical fitness which yields energy
- Emotional motivation which generates interest and focus
- Interpersonal relating which expands involvement with others
- Information relating to define operations
- Information representing to model operations
- Individual processing to generate new operations
- Interpersonal processing to generate better operations
- Interdependent processing to generate *"breakthrough"* operations

AREAS	Physical	Emotional		Intellectual				
DIMENSIONS	Physical Fitness	Personal Motivation	Interpersonal Relating	Information Relating	Information Representing	Individual Processing	Interpersonal Processing	Interdependent Processing

The Areas and Dimensions of HCD

Beyond generic predisposition, physical growth is a function primarily of diet, rest and exercise or fitness: diet sufficient to support a high level of energy output; rest sufficient to recover from that output and prepare for the next output; and fitness to *"energize"* sustained and intense output. In this book, presentation of the physical dimension will focus upon one of these factors: the fitness dimension that contributes so heavily to physical energy.

**Physical
Fitness**

Factors of Physical Growth

There are two sets of factors that define emotional growth. The first of these is the personal motivation or emotional forces that *"drive"* an individual's life activities. The second of these is interpersonal relating that disposes an individual to become involved with someone else's emotions and motivations. In other words, our motivation is *intra*personally driven and our human relations are *inter*personally driven. Together, our intrapersonal motivation and our interpersonal relations define our emotional growth and create a destiny of our own design.

Personal Motivation	**Interpersonal Relating**

Factors of Emotional Growth

There are five sets of factors that define intellectual growth. The first of these is the information relating that defines operations. The second is information representing which models operations. The third is individual processing which generates new operations. The fourth is interpersonal processing which generates better operations. The fifth is interdependent processing which generates *"breakthrough"* operations. Together these ingredients define our intellectual growth and create a *"mind"* of our own making.

Informational Learning	Individual Thinking	Interdependent Processing

Factors of Intellectual Growth

Levels of HCD

Human growth is movement from low levels of physical, emotional and intellectual functioning to high levels of physical, emotional and intellectual functioning. At the lower levels, we are passively, insensitively and intelligently productive. At the *"changeover"* or *"participation"* level, we are *"interchangeable"* in meeting the requirements of human endeavors. *Participation,* then, is the critical point of entry into the human experience. Above this level, we become increasingly human. Below this level, we are performing at less than human levels. In this context, note that there are five levels of human functioning:

- The *"detractor"* is essentially *"out-of-it"* in relating to any human endeavor.
- The *"observer"* is observant but uninvolved personally.
- The *"participant"* is fully involved.
- The *"contributor"* is *"additive"* in his or her contributions.
- The *"leader"* is highly initiative in accomplishing the goals of the endeavor.

Human Growth

The *detractor* level is a desperate level of functioning. Usually, coming from impoverished physical and psychological environments, the *detractor* may be characterized as follows:

- Physically sick and undernourished;
- Motivationally unable to respond to incentives;
- Interpersonally nonattentive to others;
- Informationally unable to define operations;
- Informationally unable to represent operations;
- Individually unable to generate new operations;
- Interpersonally unable to generate better operations;
- Interdependently unable to generate *"breakthrough"* operations.

While these descriptions are not characteristic of most people reading this material, they do define many people in the world who are under-resourced, underprivileged and disenfranchised.

The *"Detractors"*

The *observer* level is a level that may be defined as being on the verge of *"civilized behavior."* In individuals, it describes people who hold back from involvement in human endeavors, usually because of the powerful hold of their *"conditioning"* programs. The *observers* may be characterized as follows:

- Physically surviving;
- Driven by incentives;
- Oriented to attending;
- Defining concepts operationally;
- Representing operations two-dimensionally;
- Goaling individually;
- Getting others' images;
- Goaling interpersonally;
- Goaling interdependently.

The *"observing"* profile is most typical of all populations.

The *"Observers"*

The *participant* level means that the people are fully
engaged in relating to human endeavors in constructive ways. In
individuals, it describes people who are *"involved"* but not
committed to generating contributions. *Participants* may be
characterized as follows:

- Physically adaptive;
- Achievement-oriented;
- Responsive to others;
- Defining principles operationally;
- Representing operations three-dimensionally;
- Exploring operations individually;
- Sharing operations interpersonally;
- Exploring experiences interdependently.

Fully *"participative"* people are already a rare species.

The *"Participants"*

The *contributor* is a rare person who not only involves himself or herself in human endeavors but is continuously *"additive"* in contributions to these endeavors. This is the most difficult level to accomplish because it emphasizes going *"beyond the known"* dimensions of human endeavors. Accordingly, a *contributor* can be characterized as follows:

- Physically intense;
- Oriented to self-actualization;
- Capable of personalizing experiences of others;
- Defining applications operationally;
- Representing operations in nested dimensionality;
- Understanding operations individually;
- Merging operations interpersonally;
- Understanding operations interdependently.

While some rare people are oriented toward these *"contributing"* characteristics, most attempt to *"skip"* this substantive level to assume political *"leadership."*

The *"Contributors"*

"Leadership" is the logical follow-through from *"contributing." Leaders* can be characterized as follows:

- Physically enduring;
- Mission-oriented;
- Interpersonally initiative;
- Defining objectives operationally;
- Representing operations multidimensionally;
- Generating operations to act individually;
- Generating better operations to act interpersonally;
- Generating *"breakthrough"* operations to act interdependently.

Again, while some few mission-oriented people aspire to this level, we must remind ourselves that these measures of levels of human capital development are developmental and cumulative. We simply cannot skip levels. Succinctly stated, *"You can't get there from here!"*

The *"Leaders"*

The value of the HCD model is that we can *"map"* ourselves into our growth and development (Table 2). We can diagnose where we are in measurable ways. We can set objectives for where we are going with observable standards. Armed with this level of understanding, we can develop action programs to enable us to move from where we are to where we are going. We are now ready to learn the substance of HCD content.

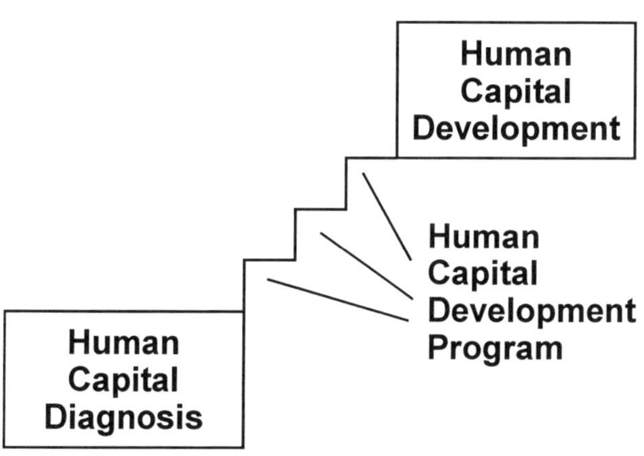

Developing an Action Plan

I. Introduction and Overview

Table 2. HUMAN CAPITAL DEVELOPMENT

LEVELS OF FUNCTIONING	PHYSICAL	EMOTIONAL		INTELLECTUAL				
	Physical Fitness	Personal Motivation	Interpersonal Relating	Information Relating	Information Representing	Individual Processing	Interpersonal Processing	Inter-dependent Processing
Leader	Stamina	Mission	Initiate	Objectives	Multi-D	Act	Go	Interdep. Acting
Contributor	Intensity	Actualize	Personalize	Applications	Nested D	Understand	Merge	Interdep. Understand.
Participant	Adapt	Achieve	Respond	Principles	3D	Explore	Give	Interdep. Exploring
Observer	Survive	Incentive	Attend	Concepts	2D	Goal	Get	Interdep. Goaling
Detractor	Sick	Non-Incentive	Non-Attending	Facts	1D	Non-Preparation	Non-Engagement	Non-Engagement

The mission of human growth, then, is to actualize the human dimensions. The human dimensions are physical, emotional and intellectual. At the highest levels of actualization, the human dimensions become qualitatively more than the sum of the parts. They *"free"* people to pursue their life's purpose. They enable people to *"throw out a skyhook"* and *"reach for the skies."* They *"empower"* people *"to pull themselves up by their own bootstraps"* to achieve their purposes. In the pages that follow, the curriculum and learnings from workplace empowering projects, *"Workforce XXI,"* will be illustrated.

Human Capital XXI

II
The HCD Ingredients

3. Physical Fitness— The Energizers

Workforce XXI is a workforce empowering project. It emphasizes empowering people with the skills, knowledge and attitudes to develop human capital for 21st century performance. To be sure, many new workforce candidates have never been employed regularly and gainfully—certainly not in positions with increasingly higher physical, emotional and intellectual requirements. Their deficits in performance may be viewed as skills deficits. The goal of any *"Workforce XXI"* program is to transform these skills deficits into skills assets. First among these deficits is physical functioning. Without high levels of physical fitness, people do not have the energy to perform in any area of their lives. With high levels of energy, people have the energy to perform productively in all areas of their lives.

Fitness → Energy

The historical orientation to fitness is straightforward. Basically, high levels of physical processing yield high levels of fitness. In other words, diet, rest and exercise transform a *"low-fit"* person into a *"high-fit"* person. The *"low-fit"* person simply does not have the energy to perform basic living, learning and working tasks while the *"high-fit"* person does.

**PHYSICAL
PROCESSING**

LOW FITNESS	DIET	REST	EXERCISE	HIGH FITNESS

Historical Context

Historically, Collingwood and others have defined the areas of fitness in terms of the following areas or categories: cardiovascular endurance or aerobic power (efficient heart and lung functioning for sustained performance); muscular strength; flexibility; and weight control, height/weight ratio, body composition or body mass measures. Together, these areas defined physical fitness. Increasing functioning in these areas increases the probability of having the energy to perform tasks.

AREAS OF FITNESS

(Collingwood and Carkhuff, 1974; Collingwood, 1992)

Endurance	Strength	Flexibility	Body Composition

Areas of Fitness

The levels of fitness were also defined. At the lowest level, sickness, the person could not survive the requirements of daily performance. At the next level, the person could barely survive. At the minimally effective level, the person could adapt to requirements. At the additive level, the person could perform with intensity. At the highest level, the person could perform with intensity and stamina.

AREAS AND LEVELS OF FITNESS

(Collingwood and Carkhuff, 1974; Collingwood, 1992)

Levels of Fitness	Endurance	Strength	Flexibility	Body Composition
5 Stamina				
4 Intensity				
3 Adaptation				
2 Survival				
1 Sickness				

Levels of Fitness

The levels of fitness were also measurable. For example, the number of tenths of a mile that could be run in twelve minutes indexed endurance or aerobic power; likewise, the number of situps performed in one minute indexed strength; the length of reach on the sit and reach test indexed flexibility; finally, the height and weight ratio indexed body composition. As may be expected, higher level functioning people run greater distances, perform more situps, have longer reach and lower body mass. Movement from one quantitative level to another is largely a matter of effort and practice.

LEVELS OF PHYSICAL FITNESS
(Collingwood and Carkhuff, 1972; Collingwood, 1992)

5	STAMINA
4	INTENSITY
3	ADAPTATION
2	SURVIVAL
1	SICKNESS

Levels of Functioning

Sickness means just that: the person is unable to survive his or her daily requirements because of a lack of fitness and energy. For example, we have found that many people required medical care before they could even participate in a physical program. The consequence of their low level of functioning was that they were already having trouble handling their current responsibilities of home and family. Yet they were considering taking on the additional burdens of learning and working. Before they could do more, they had to participate in a physical fitness program.

Sickness Level

The survival level means that people can barely survive the requirements of daily tasks. While they barely perform the tasks, they are exhausted by their energy output and this means high levels of tardiness and absenteeism in order to provide recovery time. For example, as many improved in fitness, they became satisfied that they could at least complete the tasks they set out to perform. But it was at great cost! They felt like they were on a treadmill, just barely getting one foot in front of the other in order to stand still.

Survival Level

If survival is the level at which most people function, then adaptation is the level to which most people aspire. Adaptation means that the people have energy sufficient to manage and reorganize their daily schedule as impacted by intermittent information bulletins. For example, many were pleased when they were able to handle daily events. However, they were distressed when crises arose and they found the crises demanding energies they did not have. In other words, the adaptation level did not yield the reserve energy they needed for crises.

Adaptation Level

The more energy we have, the more responsibility we may be able to handle! The more responsibility, the greater the intensity required! And, with higher levels of responsibility come greater frequencies of crises. Indeed, managers typically spend more than 50 percent of their time in crisis management. For example, as they moved up the career ladder, many found that crises were opportunities—opportunities to relate to others, opportunities to get accurate images, opportunities to negotiate solutions. Many became proud of their ability to invest their energies with intensity. Others still aspired to have energies sufficient to be intense in all areas of their lives!

Intensity Level

The highest level of physical functioning is to function with intensity and stamina. This means that people are capable of being intense in all areas of their lives. It does not mean that people cannot relax. Indeed, healthy and productive people relax with the same intensity that they invest in problem-solving, with a low pulse-rate reflecting high cardio-respiratory functioning, and high levels of energy waiting in reserve. Stamina was the level of fitness to which most people aspired. They recognized that their whole lives revolved around aperiodic crises. The rest was *"filler"* for recovery!

Stamina Level

The way to check out our aerobic power or cardiovascular *endurance* (assuming we have been medically cleared to take the test) is to see how far we can run in 12 minutes (miles and tenths). We can do the same for other areas: determine *strength* (how many bent-leg situps in one minute); *flexibility* (how far you can stretch out to or over your toes while sitting); and *body composition* (ratio of weight [in kilograms] divided by height squared [in meters]). We may look up our levels of endurance, strength, flexibility and body composition in Table 3. These ratings are meant to give a quick index of our physical functioning. A more complete picture may be developed using other sources.

LEVELS OF FITNESS	AREAS OF FITNESS			
	Endurance	**Strength**	**Flexibility**	**Body Composition**
5 **Stamina**				
4 **Intensity**				
3 **Adaptation**				
2 **Survival**				
1 **Sickness**				

Physical Profile

Table 3. PHYSICAL FITNESS NORMS
(Collingwood, 1992)

FEMALE

LEVEL	Endurance (Run)[1]	Strength (Situp)[2]	Flexibility (Stretch/Reach)[3]	Body Comp. (Ht./Wt. Index)
5 Stamina	1.6	43	8" past toes	23
4 Intensity	1.4	34	5" past toes	24
3 Adaptation	1.3	28	2" past toes	25
2 Survival	1.1	22	to toes	26
1 Non-Survival	.9	12	to ankles	27

MALE

LEVEL	Endurance (Run)[1]	Strength (Situp)[2]	Flexibility (Stretch/Reach)[3]	Body Comp. (Ht./Wt. Index)
5 Stamina	1.9	51	6" past toes	24
4 Intensity	1.7	41	3" past toes	25
3 Adaptation	1.5	36	to toes	26
2 Survival	1.3	31	to ankles	27
1 Non-Survival	1.0	22	to knees	28

1—ENDURANCE (RUN)—number of miles run in 12 minutes
2—STRENGTH (SITUPS)—number of bent-leg situps in one minute
3—FLEXIBILITY (STRENGTH & REACH)—how far you can stretch over your toes while sitting
4—BODY COMPOSITION (HEIGHT/WEIGHT RATIO)—a) divide your body weight in pounds by 2.2 to determine weight in kilograms; b) divide your height in inches by 39 to determine height in meters and tenths of a meter; c) apply the following formula to arrive at your index score:

$$\frac{\text{weight (in kilograms)}}{\text{height (in meters)}^2}$$

This means that people at the non-survival or sickness level can neither go a mile in 12 minutes; nor do more than 20 situps in one minute; or touch beyond their ankles. Furthermore, they have a very poor index of body composition or height-to-weight index. They are exhausted energy-wise. These are the most predictable of all people: they will always let everyone down—themselves and others—because they simply do not have the energy to sustain themselves. No one and nothing else really exists for them.

Non-Survival

II. The HCD Ingredients

At the survival level, people can go little more than one mile in 12 minutes; do between 20 and 30 sit-ups in one minute; touch between their ankles and their toes. They also have a poor index of body composition and resulting low levels of energy. They can be counted upon only to survive themselves at moments of crises: they simply do not have the energy to help others. They are always positioned to distance themselves from others and insulate themselves from their experience.

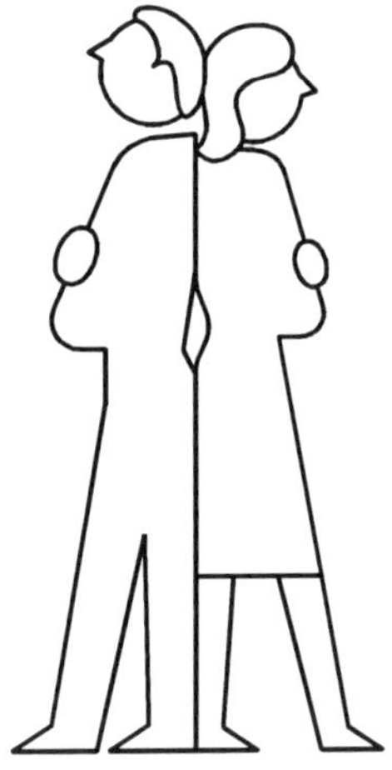

Survival

At the adaptation level, people can go nearly one and one-half miles in 12 minutes; do around 30 sit-ups; touch their toes or slightly beyond. They have moderate levels of body composition and adequate energy to adapt to their daily requirements. We may say that we can count upon them—except during moments of crises when they are needed and are too involved making standardized responses to enable themselves to adapt. They are always positioned to make minimalist responses: they *"get away clean!"*

Adaptation

At the intensity level, people can go more than one and one-half miles in 12 minutes; do more than 30 sit-ups in one minute; touch several inches beyond their toes. They have good body composition and energy. They can be counted upon to respond with intense periodic *"spikes"* to customize solutions for themselves and others. They are always positioned to embrace the experiences of their loves ones.

Intensity

At the stamina level, people can go nearly two miles in 12 minutes; do more than 40 sit-ups in one minute; touch more than one-half foot beyond their toes. Their body composition and their energy reservoirs are excellent. They can be counted upon to respond with stamina to create tailored solutions for themselves and a continuously expanding group of significant others. They are positioned to embrace the universe of human experiences.

Stamina

We may obtain our modal level of physical functioning in the various areas of life activities: home, school, work, organization and community by simply assessing the level of fitness at which we appear most often across areas of functioning. This level represents the degree to which we have developed our physical functions.

LEVELS OF FITNESS	AREAS OF APPLICATION				
	Home	School	Work	Org.	Community
5 Stamina					
4 Intensity					
3 Adaptation					
2 Survival					
1 Sickness					

Modal Physical Profile

It is important to emphasize that we progress developmentally and cumulatively through the levels of fitness just as a child progresses in human development. This means that each level of fitness becomes a necessary condition for the next level. In this context, the goal of fitness is to provide a level of energy sufficient to function with intensity and stamina. In other words, the goal of fitness is to live life fully. Perhaps most importantly, the physical realm gives us a prototype for assessing ourselves in all other realms. While the normative data with which to compare ourselves may not be so clear in other areas of functioning, the physical realm pushes us very hard with clear-cut criteria. Either we can run a mile in seven minutes or we cannot. We cannot delude ourselves from day-to-day and year-to-year. Although we may feel "good" temporarily, there are long-term implications to a deteriorating physical condition for other dimensions of human capital. In the long run, we cannot actualize our human capital potential without the continuous support of our physical fitness and the physical energy that it serves to facilitate.

Physical Perspective

We must take responsibility for elevating our own levels of physical functioning. This means an ongoing learning program about nutrition, rest and exercise, and an active personal physical development program. We must also support and promote physical goals for others, as we fulfill our responsibilities as parents, leaders and members of organizations, and as citizens.

Physical Responsibility

To sum, physical fitness is the great energizer. However *"professional"* they appear during calm times, *"low-fit"* people are characterized by an inability to mobilize to produce energy when it is required of them. Conversely, however calm they appear during calm times, *"high-fit"* people are characterized by the ability to produce energy when it is necessary. Without fitness, people may not be available in time of crisis: they may not be motivated to expend effort, not able to relate to expand experience, not able to be generative to explode with new ideas. With fitness, people are able to mobilize their emotions and their intellects in times of crisis. In short, without fitness, *"nothing"* is possible! With fitness, *"everything"* is possible!

The Energizers

4. Personal Motivation— The Catalyzers

Perhaps the greatest obstacle to succeeding with a *"Workforce XXI"* project is the lack of motivation of the candidates. Many of the candidates simply have never been rewarded for any efforts in their lives—not at home, not at school, not at work! They have been placed by the system on what psychologists term *"extinction schedules:"* that is, their ability to mobilize industrious responses has been *"extinguished"* by the lack of positive reinforcements. The goal of any human capital empowering program is to mobilize the candidates' motivation. As the candidates will discover, high levels of motivation yield high levels of commitment in performing productively in all areas of their lives.

Motivation → Commitment

The real issue, then, is how to relate job requirements to personal values to produce motivation. In this context, external incentives are only one way to motivate performance. In order to understand individuals' motives, we need to empathically enter their frames of reference, and then relate performance reinforcements to their frames of reference. *"Motivation"* is a product of relating reinforcements to values and requirements in such a way as to introduce hope for future rewards and benefits.

Motivation was first put in perspective by Maslow. His theory emphasized five basic needs arranged in a hierarchical fashion. At the bottom of the hierarchy were the most basic physiological needs. In an ascending order of significance, security, social, ego and self-actualization needs came into play. Once a person's needs were satisfied at one level, he or she moved up to the next level of needs.

MASLOW'S HIERARCHY OF NEEDS (1954)

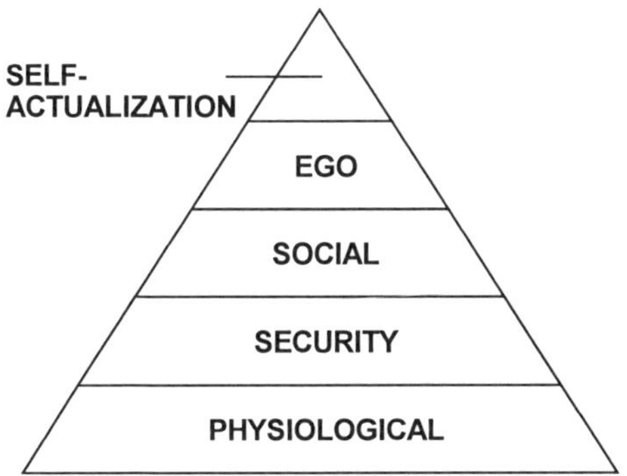

Historical Context

Herzberg later modified Maslow's theory to emphasize two sets of motivational factors. The first of these, *"dissatisfiers,"* cause dissatisfaction if not present. Thus, poor relationships, benefits or working conditions could demotivate the potential worker or learner. The second set of factors, *"motivators,"* could contribute to satisfaction and lead to an internal push to do well. Thus, achievement or work itself, in addition to responsibility, advancement and recognition could motivate people.

HERZBERG'S ANALYSIS OF MOTIVATORS AND DISSATISFIERS (1966)

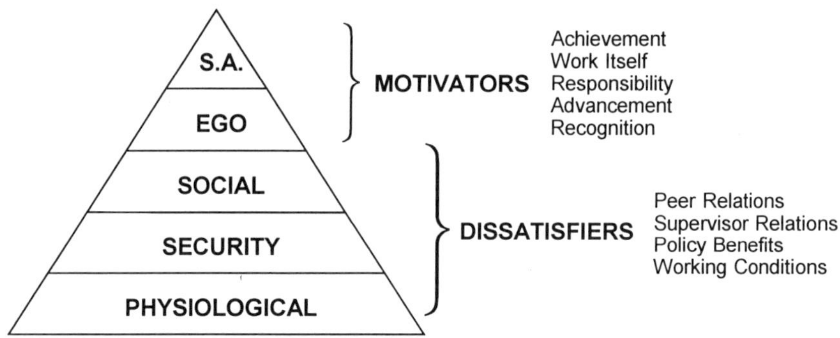

Generative Contributions

Our own work led us to a description of motivation in terms of functional levels of reinforcing experiences. The non-incentive level meant that people were not responding to reinforcements of any kind. The incentive level meant that people responded to reinforcements—whether of a physiological, security or social nature. The achievement level reflects ego-reinforcing pride in craftsmanship. The self-actualization level emphasizes personal fulfillment and accomplishment. The mission level emphasizes a personal mission outside of one's own ego boundaries.

LEVELS OF MOTIVATION
(Carkhuff, 1983)

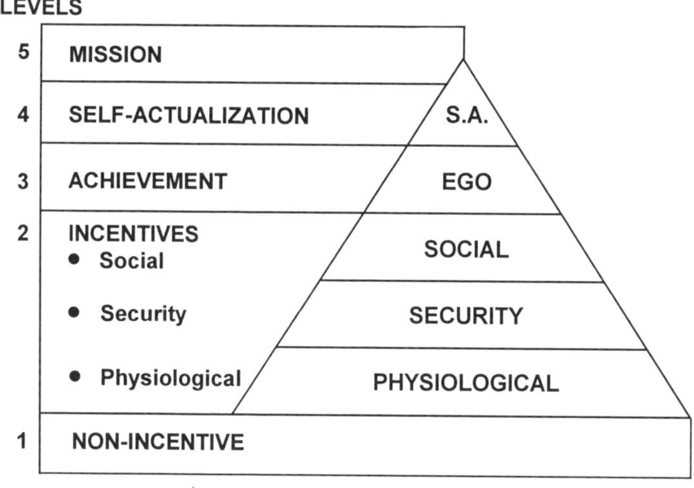

Levels of Motivation

II. The HCD Ingredients

The source of motivation is emotional. In all of life's experiences, an individual's emotion-based values interact with environmental or market requirements. It is easy to see in the experience of an individual processing career values in relation to job requirements. In healthy individuals, motivational goals are a negotiated product of processing or thinking to maximize meeting both requirements and values. Thus, in the context of different environmental requirements, the emotional values are transformed into different motivational goals. When this occurs, we may think of ourselves as functioning at different levels of *"emotivation."*

Relating Emotion to Motivation

The levels of emotivation, then, range from the non-incentive level through external incentives to internal motivators such as a need to achieve, or a drive for self-actualization, to people with missions outside of themselves. These levels are developmental and cumulative: people at the higher levels outperform people at the lower levels by wide margins in all areas of human endeavor.

LEVELS OF MOTIVATION
(Carkhuff, 1992)

5	**MISSION**
4	**ACTUALIZATION**
3	**ACHIEVEMENT**
2	**INCENTIVE**
1	**NON-INCENTIVE**

Levels of Motivation

II. The HCD Ingredients

At the non-incentive level, people are not part of the incentive system as we know it. They may have operated within a system and been rejected by it or, conversely, they may have rejected it. Or they may be part of a system to which we are not attuned: for example, the incentive system provided by the criminal career ladder. Nevertheless, people at this non-incentive level can be motivated by people who enter their frames of reference in order to determine what is reinforcing for them. Generally, reinforcements at this level emphasize immediate and sometimes idiosyncratic reinforcements. For example, we have found that some employees worked if certain conditions were met: being picked up and delivered to work; allowed to arrive and leave at convenient but irregular hours; allowed to work with reduced workloads; given regular work breaks and nourishment; paid immediately (initially this may mean the day of the effort). Generally, people at this level have failed to respond to incentives because no one has responded empathically to them.

Non-Incentive Level

The incentive level is traditionally conceived of as motivation. Generally, people are controlled by reinforcement schedules determined by others. Here people work to receive external, secondary reinforcers such as money, promotions, leisure time and the like. For example, we found that while incentive-driven people do what is necessary to receive rewards, they are concerned only with satisfying the standards of the manipulators of the reinforcement system. They assume no initiative for producing products or delivering services that might be of benefit to the organization or to other people within it. In Herzberg's terms, incentives are potential *"dissatisfiers"* which, if not satisfied, demotivate performance. Again, incentives, like all other reinforcements, depend, for their potency, upon accurately empathizing with the recipient's frame of reference.

Incentive Level

While incentives may be necessary, they are not a sufficient condition for motivating many people. At the achievement level, people function to fulfill their need for success. Included in this need are attributes of pride in performance or craftsmanship. In general, achievers are productive people who follow the initiatives of others. For example, in our own work we have found that people came to feel cheated of meaning in their lives when they realized that others were experiencing the satisfaction of achievement and they were not. They learned to make great investments in maximizing the quality of their products and in minimizing the impact of more traditional incentives.

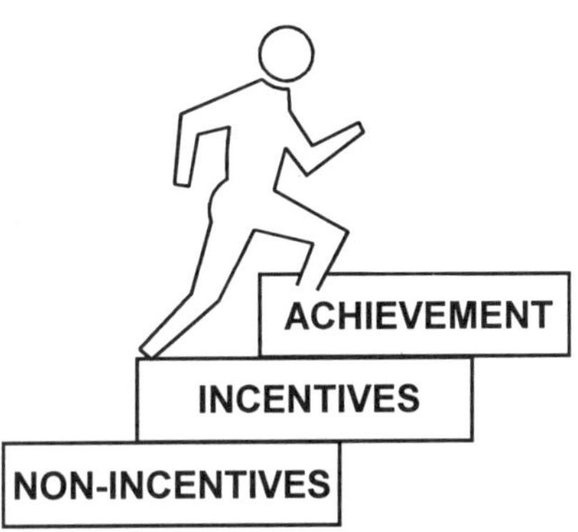

Achieving Level

At the next highest level of motivation, actualizing, people are concerned with fulfilling themselves. For people interested in actualizing themselves, the motivator is *"opportunity."* Above all else, the actualizers want the opportunities to acquire and apply new skills, knowledge and attitudes. For actualizers, the mission is inside, rather than outside of themselves. In all situations, they are oriented toward learning in order to grow fully. In our own work, for example, trainees found that the idea of personal growth gave meaning to their lives: they began to develop themselves socially and intellectually; they began to see their work as a by-product of their own human capital development.

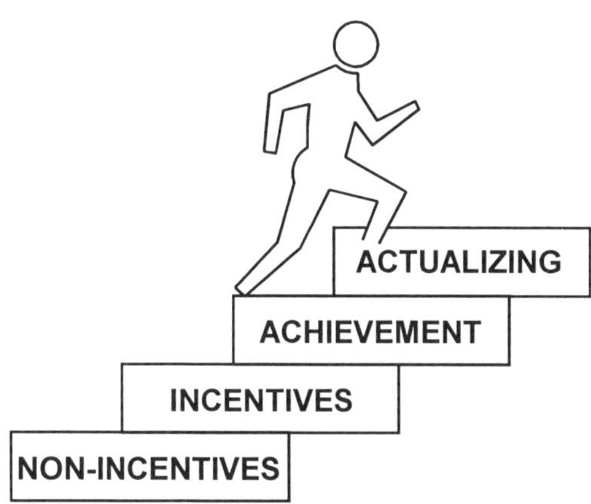

Actualizing Level

II. The HCD Ingredients

At the highest level of motivation, people have missions outside of themselves that give meaning to their lives. These are not missions to which they have been conditioned by child-rearing or corporate indoctrination. They are missions that they have discovered in their own growth experiences. These missions usually culminate in growth benefits for others. For example, some people find missions that are consistent with organizational or community or spiritual organizations. These guiding missions usually culminate in growth benefits for others. These guiding missions also enable people to relate all of the tasks in their daily existence to fulfilling their missions. Everything has meaning in their lives and their work. All growth missions involve nurturing life forces wherever and whenever they are encountered.

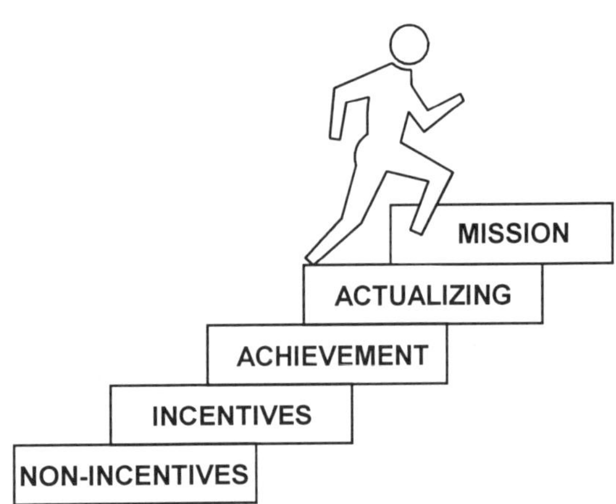

Missioning Level

One way of checking our own level of intrapersonal motivation is to plot ourselves in terms of our daily living. To qualify at any one of these levels of functioning, we must have engaged in at least one act or behavior daily within each of our areas of functioning. Thus, to qualify for the incentive level, we must have fulfilled one or more daily objectives that are consistent with our being rewarded or with our avoidance of punishment. To qualify at the achievement level, we must have accomplished one or more daily objectives that yield our pride in accomplishment. To qualify at the level of actualizing ourselves, we must have initiated one or more times beyond our daily objectives to find fulfillment in our lives. To qualify for a mission outside of ourselves, we must have completed one or more objectives, daily, to serve that mission. While the daily requirements are stringent, they emphasize our "way of life." If we are not involved in the behaviors of a given emotivational level on a daily basis, then we are not functioning at that level.

LEVELS OF MOTIVATION

5   MISSION

4   ACTUALIZATION

3   ACHIEVEMENT

2   INCENTIVE

1   NON-INCENTIVE

Motivational Profile

The non-incentive level does not mean that people function-ing at this level do not have any incentives in their lives. It sim-ply means that no one attempting to influence their performance has discovered their incentives. In this respect, the people are dependent upon others to motivate them. They may also be reac-tive to their own dependency: rejecting the attempts made by others to motivate them with incentives. Non-incentive-driven people will not do the job.

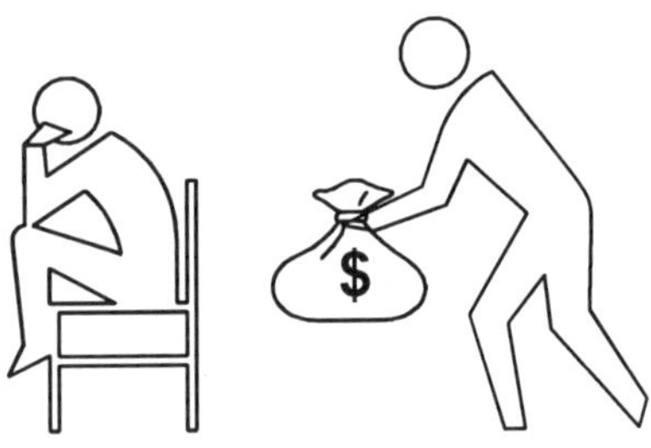

Non-Incentive

The incentive level means that people do respond to incentives. These incentives may be standardized, such as financial rewards, or they may be personalized to the frames of reference of the people. These incentives motivate the people to perform; they may even motivate the people to perform better in order to obtain more rewards. Incentive-driven people will do the job.

Incentive

The achievement level means that people are motivated by their achievements. With products, people may be motivated by *"pride in craftsmanship."* In business, people may be motivated by producing the best products or delivering the best services on-time and at the cheapest prices. In their personal lives, people may be motivated by their own personal achievements such as those reflected in performance indicators and milestones. Achievement-driven people will do the job well.

Achieving

The actualizing level means that people are motivated by the prospects of actualizing their own potential. They have a large perspective of their potential contributions. While they perform at high levels in any one area, they view their performance in relation to their overall potential. Thus, for example, they may actualize their potential in all of their resources: physically energized, emotionally catalyzed, intellectually actualized. Actualization-driven people do everything at the highest levels: they expect nothing less from themselves.

Actualizing

The missioning level means that people are motivated by a mission beyond themselves. They have discovered the central meaning in their lives and have become *"one"* with it. This mission can be as different as personal value systems. Parents may have missions of rearing children to fulfill their potential. Teachers may have missions of empowering learners with tools to maximize their performance. Managers may have missions to fulfill the organization's contribution to maximizing productivity, growth and profit. Mission-driven people dedicate their lives to the performance of all elements contributing to the fulfillment of the mission.

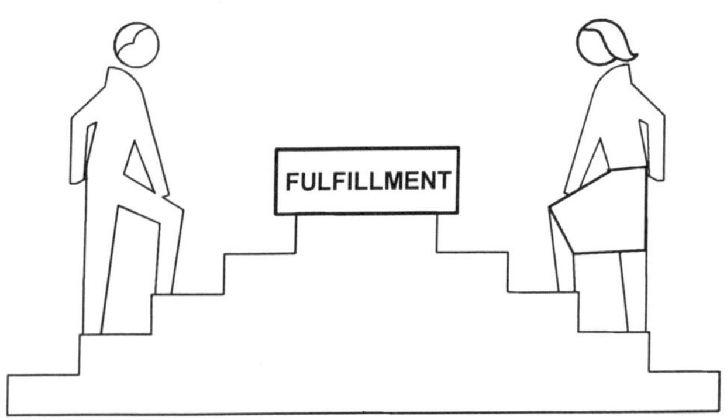

Missioning

Again, for rating motivation, we obtain the modal level of functioning or the level at which we function most frequently. Included are modal levels for different areas of functioning. These areas include our functioning at home, in continuing education, at work, and in the community. In our experience, some people slide up and down this scale, at different points being committed to different motives. Just the fact that a person is driven by a mix of motivations implies that this person is functioning, subliminally, at the lowest of these motivation levels. Again, we may most effectively assess the level of motivation by determining an individual's modal level of functioning. In practice, humans often use high principles and unselfish motives when the decision does not matter, and then get down to "nitty-gritty" incentives when it does. It is valid that survival must be assured before growth can take place. However, in the end, those who do not get outside of themselves in their motivation do not actualize their human capital potential.

Levels of Motivation	Areas of Application				
	Home	School	Work	Org.	Community
5 Mission					
4 Actualization					
3 Achievement					
2 Incentive					
1 Non-Incentive					

Modal Motivational Profile

It is our experience that healthy and growthful persons move developmentally through the levels of motivation. Just as one cannot actualize human potential without meeting certain physical and emotional preconditions, so one cannot be motivated at the highest levels without having worked through the earlier levels. Thus, the healthy and productive person relates all of the other levels of motivation to his or her highest levels. In this context, there are conditions under which he or she responds to incentives and achievement as well as to conditions for not doing so. However, all of these motivational responses are related to fulfilling missions both inside and outside of oneself. And, ultimately, it is the servicing of these missions of self-actualization and human benefit that catalyzes our resources.

Motivational Perspective

In order to intentionally elevate motivations from one level to another, we must first grasp an understanding of motivational operations. For the currently non-motivated, we provide differential reinforcements, specific to the individual involved. This may mean very close and intimate supervision of performance as well as immediate dispensation of reinforcements. For those motivated by incentives we provide external rewards, at first immediate, then delayed. For the achievement-oriented person, we must enter his or her frame of reference in order to support his or her internal achievement reinforcers. For the self-actualizer, we provide time and opportunities. For those motivated by mission, we provide freedom and resources to pursue missions beyond current mandates. This motivational scale undergirds all our initiatives in elevating motivation, others as well as our own.

Motivational Skills

To sum, motivation is the catalyst for performance. In this respect, it is really a cost-beneficial question. It is the price we are willing to pay for the benefits to which we aspire. If our efforts and benefits are integrated, then our motivation catalyzes our behavior. As we mature in our motivation, we are less the prisoner of external reinforcements or incentives and more the initiator of our own internal reinforcements. In other words, we internalize responsibility for the quality of our products (achievement), the quality of our person (actualization), and the quality of the world around us (mission). In the final analysis, motivation and performance are synergistically related in a spiraling cycle of growth moving from external reinforcements to internal commitments.

The Catalyzers

5. Interpersonal Relating—
The Facilitators

Perhaps the most critical ingredient in empowering candidates in a *"Workforce XXI"* project is interpersonal relating.
Many of the candidates are unable to relate to their worlds and
the people in them. This is often because no one ever related to
their frames of reference. They are trapped inside of their *"own
skins,"* unable to identify with another person, let alone fellow
workers, supervisors or organizations. The goal of any
"Workforce XXI" project is to empower the candidates to relate to
their worlds. As the candidates will discover, high levels of
interpersonal relating skills yield high levels of relationships
with an increasingly expanding world.

Interpersonal Skills → Relating

Indeed, high levels of interpersonal skills serve another critical relating purpose: facilitating the functioning of others. By relating to the frames of reference of others, the interpersonal skills help us to facilitate relationships—*"up, down and sideways"*:

- *"Up"*—by sharing images of tasks with supervisors
- *"Down"*—by sharing images of tasks with subordinates
- *"Sideways"*—by sharing images of tasks with peers and fellow workers

Relating skills are the critical ingredients in all team-building and organizing relationships.

Relating → Facilitating

Just as relating leads to facilitating, so does facilitating lead to relating. Historically, it was known as *"the golden rule":* that we treat others the way we would like to be treated. In *"Workforce XXI,"* we label it the principle of *"reciprocal relating":* people tend to relate to us in the same manner that we have related to them. That is precisely why it is so important for trainers, teachers and helpers to relate facilitatively to trainees, learners and helpees. It is incumbent upon the more skilled person to facilitate and then empower the other person in relating skills. As they become empowered with interpersonal relating skills, the workforce members will discover a whole new world of experience—human and otherwise—unfolding to them.

Facilitating → Relating

Indeed, it is precisely these interpersonal relating skills that are critical to all human relationships at all levels of maturity. Interpersonal skills facilitate the phases of human learning or processing—*"Exploring, Understanding and Acting."*

- *Exploring is facilitated, as all learning begins with the learners' frames of reference;*
- *Understanding is facilitated, as all learning must be instrumental for the learners' purposes or goals;*
- *Acting is facilitated, as all learning must incorporate step-by-step procedures to move from the learners' frames of reference to their goals.*

The phases of learning or processing—*"Exploring, Understanding and Acting"*—serve to guide our movement through the interpersonal phases of facilitating or relating.

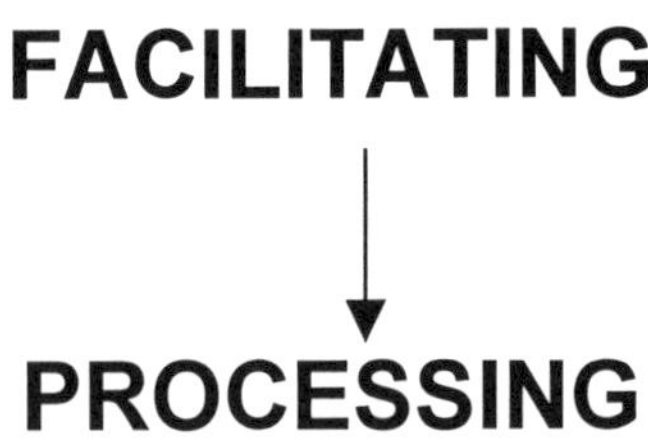

Interpersonal Relating

The study of interpersonal skills is a largely American phenomenon, beginning a little over a half-century ago with the Freudians and Neo-Freudians: they theorized that early interpersonal relations provided a paradigm for *understanding* adult experiences. Building upon these contributions, the Client-Centered and Existential approaches emphasized a non-directive orientation as the source of *exploring* these experiences. Simultaneously, the Trait-and-Factor theorists and the Behaviorists emphasized highly programmatic methods for *acting* upon these experiences. With research, it became apparent that each of these mutually exclusive schools was inadequate to account for human experience. Indeed, it was only when they were placed together in an integrated model for interpersonal relations that they made contributions to human relating and human growth.

INTERPERSONAL EMPHASIS OF DIFFERENT APPROACHES
(Carkhuff & Berenson, 1967)

EXPLORING	UNDERSTANDING	ACTING
Client-Centered, Existential	Psychoanalytic, Neo-Analytic	Trait-and-Factor, Behaviorist

Historical Context

Drawing largely from these differing orientations, we integrated skills programs in a comprehensive model for human relating. The early Trait-and-Factor approaches were historical sources of attending skills. The Client-Centered and Existential approaches stimulated the development of empathic responding skills. The Freudian and Neo-Freudian approaches provided rich resources for conceptualizing personalizing skills. Finally, the Trait-and-Factor approaches oriented us to define objectives in operational dimensions and the Behavioristic approaches contributed to the development of step-by-step initiative programs. Together, the new skills programs empowered a person to facilitate another's movement through the phases of learning or processing: involvement in relating; exploration of experience; understanding of problems and goals; and the development of action programs.

PHASES OF INTERPERSONAL SKILLS
(Carkhuff, 1972)

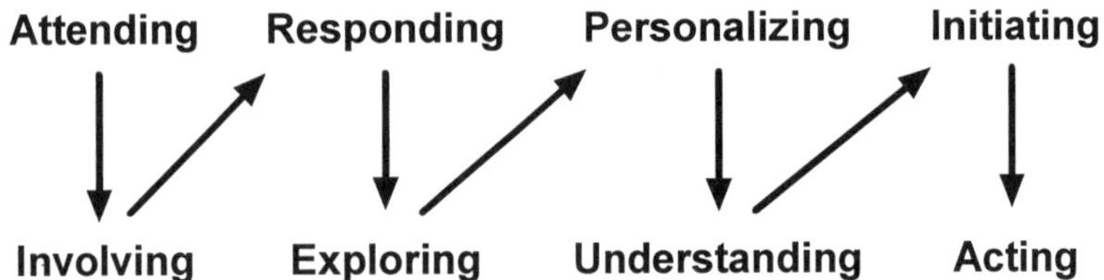

Generative Contributions

The key to operationalizing interpersonal skills, we found, was in formulating the *"interchangeable response."* The interchangeable response (Level 3) meant that the relator or helper captured the feeling and meaning of the verbal and behavioral expressions of the recipient or helpee. In other words, the expressions of both parties could be laid side-by-side and the following question answered: Could the helper have said what the helpee said, and vice versa? The developmental stages leading up to empathic responsiveness emphasized the "hovering attentiveness" of attending (Level 2). The developmental stages, building upon empathic responsiveness, emphasized personalizing the helpee's goals (Level 4) and initiating to develop courses of action (Level 5).

LEVELS OF INTERPERSONAL RELATIONS
(Carkhuff, 1992)

5	INITIATING
4	PERSONALIZING
3	RESPONDING
2	ATTENDING
1	NON-ATTENTIVENESS

Levels of IPS

Non-attending simply means that people are inattentive to one another. They really do not get involved because they really are not paying attention. This means that they cannot get *"inside"* another person's experience. Indeed, in many respects, they do not even stand *"outside"* in relation to others. They place all kinds of barriers in the way of entering a communication process with another person. They may even play the role of *"paying attention"* but it is a *"frozen posture"* without a real person observing and listening. For example, even before training, many supervisors understood the risks of functioning at a non-attentive level because it deprived them of the most basic information about their employees.

Non-Attending Level

Initially, the most difficult human relations skills to get people to apply are the skills needed to attend to another person. Resistance to the application of attending skills is encountered in many ways. Basically, however, people are saying, *"I'm just not comfortable that way."* Whether or not being attentive helps them to look at and *"see"* others, and listen and *"hear"* them, does not matter. They are simply caught up in themselves and unable to relate to others by attending: physically—by posturing themselves to pay attention; or observationally—by observing the appearance and behavior of others; or auditorally—by listening to the expressions of others. For example, supervisors found that they learned much of what they needed to know about their employees by *"seeing"* and *"hearing"* them.

Attending Level

At minimally effective levels of relating, people are responding accurately to the expressions of others. They are at least able to communicate their understanding of the other's expressions. This includes capturing the gist of the content; inferring the feeling behind the content; and integrating the feeling and content into a response that has meaning for the other person. With this *"interchangeable level"* of understanding, productive human relations are possible. Without responding accurately, nothing is possible! For example, supervisors found that responding accurately to others was the lever to facilitate the employees' exploration of tasks to perform and problems to solve.

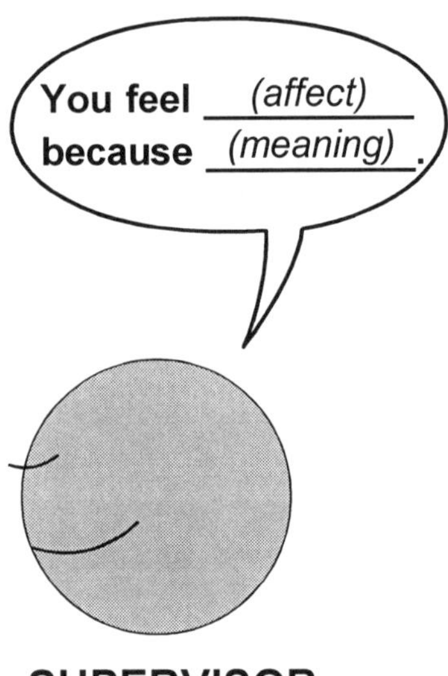

SUPERVISOR

Responding Level

Personalizing is the most complex interpersonal skill. It emphasizes helping the other person to internalize responsibility for his or her experience. Usually, it culminates in some level of disappointment for some acknowledged responsibility in failing. It means that the other person is "owning" a role in his or her experience. At the highest levels, personalizing will generate a course of action. For example, supervisors find that by personalizing their responses to employees, they facilitate employees' understanding of their goals.

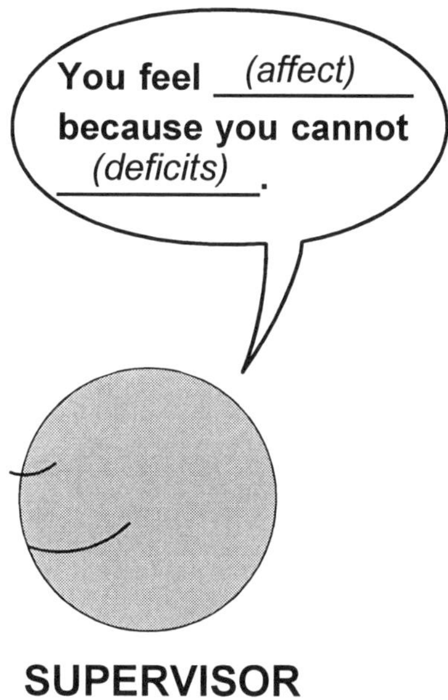

Personalizing Level

Initiating is the culminating ingredient of human relating. It means that we not only respond accurately to where people are and help them to personalize their understanding of where they want or need to be, but we also work with them to initiate individualized action programs to get them there. We do this by operationally defining objectives and systematically developing action programs to achieve the objectives. For example, supervisors find that by initiating with their employees, they facilitate individualized action programs to resolve problems and achieve goals.

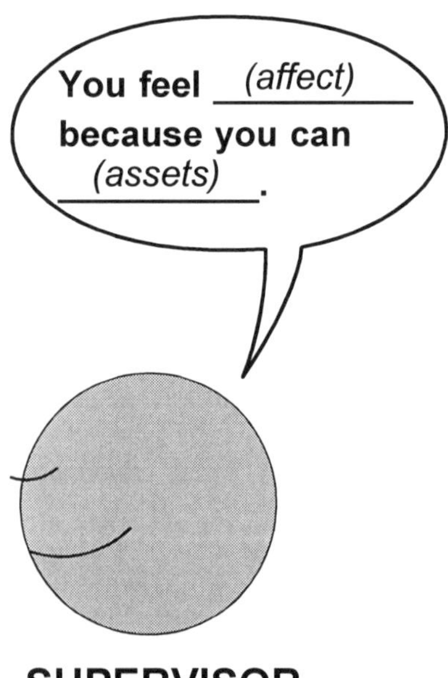

Initiating Level

One way of checking our own level of interpersonal relations is to plot ourselves in terms of our daily living. Again, to qualify at any one of these levels of functioning, we must have engaged in at least one act daily within each area of functioning. Thus, to qualify at the attending level, we must have given our full and undivided attention to the appropriate people one or more times on a daily basis. For responding, we must have communicated interchangeably to the expressions of significant others at least once each day. Personalizing requires responding to help others identify and "own" a goal. To qualify, we must personalize for each significant person at least once each day. Initiating demands that we help to develop an action course for each significant person at least once each day. If we do not apply these interpersonal skills on a daily basis, we do not have them.

LEVELS OF INTERPERSONAL SKILLS

5   **INITIATING**

4   **PERSONALIZING**

3   **RESPONDING**

2   **ATTENDING**

1   **NON-ATTENDING**

Interpersonal Skills Profile

The non-attending level means that we are not paying attention to others. We may be caught up in our own thoughts or work. Or we may simply not have skills to attend. In any event, we learn nothing from the other person.

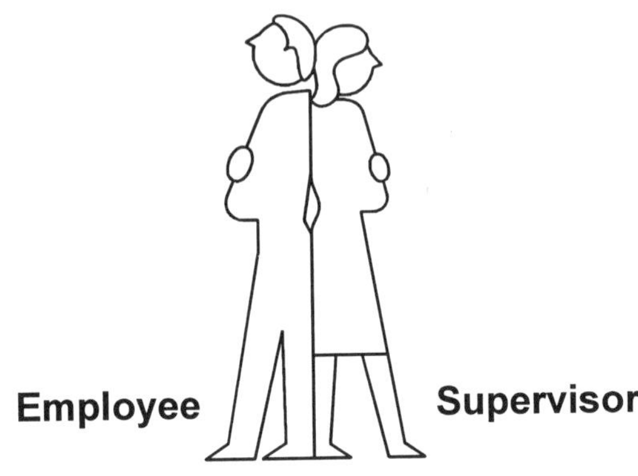

Non-Attending

The attending level means that we are paying attention to the other person. This serves to communicate a *"hovering attentiveness"* to them as well as to maximize our learning about them. We learn most of what we need to know through our senses: viewing and *"seeing"* their appearance and behavior; listening and *"hearing"* the content and affect of their expressions.

Attending

II. The HCD Ingredients

The responding level is the critical threshold to interpersonal relating. This serves to both discriminate and communicate our understanding. We discriminate by *"hearing"* the music (affect) as well as the words (content). We communicate by making responses that are interchangeable with the words and music. This interchangeability of communication establishes a platform for continuous learning for all parties.

Responding

Personalizing establishes a basis for internalizing responsibility for deficits as well as assets in performance. It is this *"ownership"* of behavior that motivates people to go on to improve their behavior. It is this *"ownership"* of behavior that impels people to life-long change.

Personalizing

Initiating means that people are acting upon their personalized responses to improve their performance. They are developing and implementing systematic programs to grow. There is no understanding without action; no growth without steps; no change without initiative.

Initiating

The same approach is appropriate to rating ourselves at those levels at which we function most of the time. Thus, we are rated at the modal level of our functioning at home, school, work, organization and in the community. It is noteworthy that those of us who achieve the highest or deepest levels of human relations are always monitoring our levels of understanding by responding interchangeably with other peoples' experiences. People who do not have deepening human relations in any arena are never responding accurately to the experiences of others. And, all human relations are in the process of deepening or deteriorating! Those whose relationships are deteriorating cannot actualize their human potential. Those whose relationships are deepening can expand their humanity and actualize their humanity and, ultimately, actualize their human capital potential.

Levels of Interpersonal Relating	Areas of Application				
	Home	School	Work	Org.	Community
5 Initiating					
4 Personalizing					
3 Responding					
2 Attending					
1 Non-Attending					

Modal Interpersonal Skills Profile

Again, the growthful human facilitator moves developmentally through the levels of relating: attending to facilitate involvement; responding to facilitate exploring; personalizing to facilitate understanding; initiating to facilitate acting. Interpersonal relations are preconditions for all interdependency. If we cannot relate to others, then we cannot process productively with them—for any purpose! In the final analysis, the great facilitator is interpersonal skills. There is no productive action without empathic understanding; and no empathic understanding without productive action!

Interpersonal Perspective

Understand that the expressed need for interpersonal relating skills is a relatively recent phenomena. Learning to relate interpersonally is a critical step that humanity must take as the world's diverse populations live and work side-by-side. Currently, available interpersonal skills training varies in quality. Most programs teach physical attending, observation, listening and paraphrasing content skills (less than Level 3). We must, however, acquire and apply the skills of responding (Level 3), personalizing (Level 4) and initiating (Level 5) if we are to actualize our relations with others.

Interpersonal Skills

To sum, the interpersonal dimensions serve as facilitators for all growth. As we relate to others' internal frames of reference, we serve to facilitate their growth. For one thing, others realize that someone else can share their experience and, thus, they recognize the commonality of their humanity. In the process, the facilitator becomes a potent reinforcer and, therefore, a catalyst for growth. Moreover, as we relate to others, we expand the boundaries of our own human experience and in so doing, facilitate our own growth. In short, all learning begins with the learner's frame of reference. The interpersonal ability to enter another's frame of reference is the source of all growth.

The Facilitators

6. Information Relating— The Operationalizers

Where relating is the lever that expands human experience, learning is an application of relating. Learning is relating to information. We enter the world of information just as we enter the world of humans: by attending, responding, personalizing and initiating. In our *"Workforce XXI"* projects, we transfer the skills of relating to people to relating to information. Information provides the basic building blocks of processing or thinking. To be sure, information is both the input and output of processing. Therefore, information provides the criteria by which we may judge the productivity of our processing.

Relating → Information

II. The HCD Ingredients

We have not entered the frame of reference of information until we have understood its content. In other words, content represents the internal experience of information. For example, in the *"Workforce XXI"* projects, we teach candidates how to read the page of a book: first, identifying the facts or data elements; next, building the concepts or relationships between data points; then, developing the principles or explanations of the relationships; then, defining the objectives to be achieved; finally, developing programs to achieve the objectives.

Information → Content

Further, in our *HC XXI* projects, we have not personalized our understanding of the content until we have understood the operations defining the content. The basic building blocks of information are the dimensions of all operations: the functions, components, processes, conditions and standards of content. As the candidates become empowered with information and learning skills, the HCD candidates will discover the power of building information for their own purposes.

Content → Operations

Bloom addressed intellectual learning in a taxonomy of educational objectives in a cognitive domain. He was primarily concerned with analyzing the learning tasks of content as they applied to the more abstract goals of instruction. Bloom's model is a descriptive one. For Bloom, *knowledge* deals with the recall of information and *comprehension* with the understanding of material. In turn, *application* emphasizes concrete demonstrations of abstract knowledge. *Analysis* involves breaking a phenomenon into its parts, while *synthesis* involves putting the elements into a whole. Finally, *evaluation* involves judging the material for a given purpose. While offering an entry into the area of cognition, unfortunately, the taxonomy mixes processing dimensions such as analysis, synthesis and evaluation with content dimensions such as knowledge, comprehension and application.

BLOOM'S TAXONOMY
OF COGNITION (1956)

6   EVALUATION

5   SYNTHESIS

4   ANALYSIS

3   APPLICATION

2   COMPREHENSION

1   KNOWLEDGE

Historical Content

In our work, we sought to separate the content from its processing. Consequently, we developed levels of intellectual content which range from facts to programs. At that time, *facts* were identified as the names or labels—usually nouns—that identify *what* a thing is. *Concepts* were defined by the meanings—usually adjectives, verbs or adverbs—we attach to things that tell us about them and *what* they do. In turn, *principles* were defined by the relationships within and between facts and concepts that tell us *how* and why a thing does what it does. Applications were defined by the contexts or environments that tell us *where* and *when* the things happen. Objectives were defined by the operations that make the things achievable and tell us *how well* we have done.

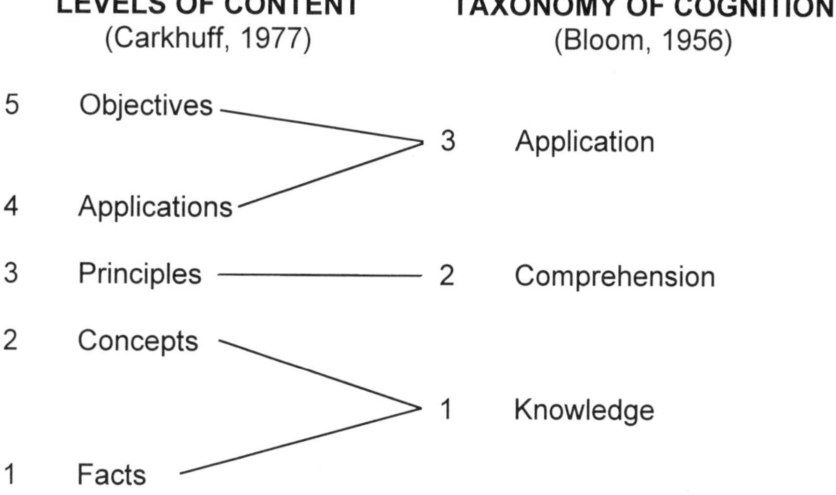

Generative Contributions

II. The HCD Ingredients

Dissatisfied with these still conceptual definitions of the content, we further operationalized our language system; that way we could relate each level of information developmentally and operationally. Moreover, we could then train anyone in the basic operational language skills required for systematic intellectual processing. Thus, facts are the names we attach to components and functions. Concepts are the relationships within and between these components and functions that give meaning to the facts. Principles are processes that explain the relationships between and among the components and functions. Applications are the conditions for processing. Objectives are the operations and standards for processing. The pages that follow will further describe these levels of intellectual content.

LEVEL OF INTELLECTUAL LEARNING
(Carkhuff, 1992)

5   OBJECTIVES

4   APPLICATIONS

3   PRINCIPLES

2   CONCEPTS

1   FACTS

Levels of Intellectual Learning

Webster defines a fact as a deed or act—*"a thing that has actually happened or is really true."* In this context, we may conceive of facts as data elements. More operationally, we may think of them as components and functions. Components are the parts or participants of a phenomenon. They answer the question, *"What or who is involved?"* In turn, functions are the actions or activities of the phenomenon. They answer the question, *"What is being done?"* Together, components and functions define the data elements of any phenomena. For example, an employee may find facts empowering when he or she can identify the components and functions of a machine that he or she is operating.

FACTS OR DATA

COMPONENTS, FUNCTIONS

Facts

Concepts are conceived by Webster as *"ideas or thoughts, especially generalized ideas of a class of objects."* We may conceive of concepts as the relationships between data elements that define phenomena. When any data element is related to any other data element, we have a concept of their relationship. Operationally, this means that components may be related to functions and other components. Likewise, functions may be related to components and other functions. Concepts answer the question, *"What is being related?"* These relationships go beyond independent data elements to define the first forms of related information. For example, an employee may find concepts particularly helpful in identifying relationships between components and functions—the relationships of nouns and verbs along with modifying adjectives, adverbs and related phrases.

CONCEPTS OR RELATIONSHIPS

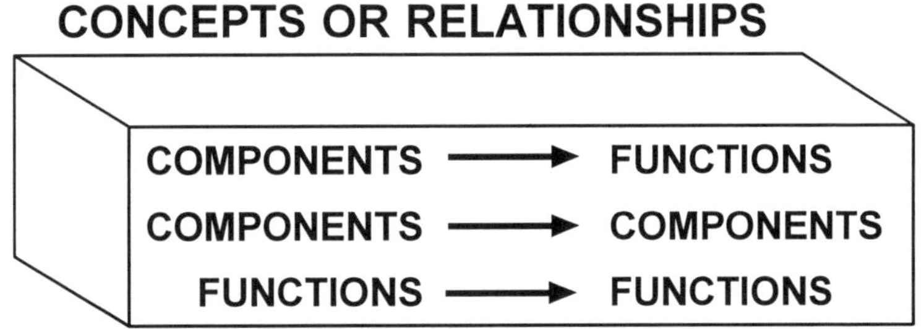

Concepts

Principles are viewed by Webster as *"the ultimate source, origin, or cause of something."* We may conceive of principles as explanations for phenomena. These explanations are the processes or procedures or methods that enable the data elements to be transformed. Operationally, for example, this means that the processes enable the components to discharge functions. Processes answer the questions, *"Why and how do the phenomena take place?"* These explanations define the first forms of knowledge. For example, principles may empower an employee to understand both the procedures and the explanations, the *how* and *why*, of information.

PRINCIPLES OR EXPLANATIONS

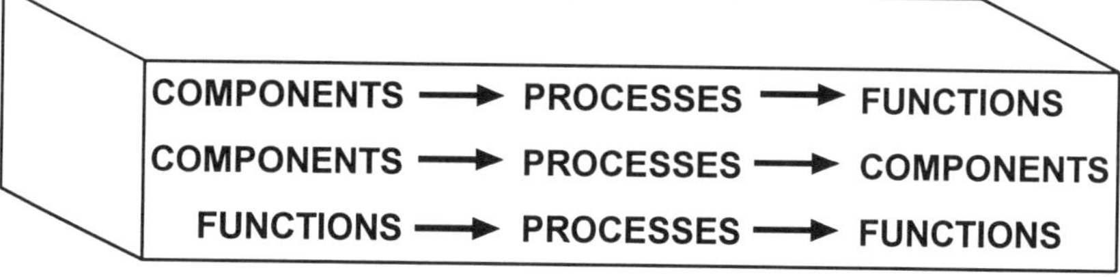

Principles

II. The HCD Ingredients

Applications have been conceived historically as things that we wish to accomplish. In other words, applications define the conditions of our processes. These conditions are described by the context or environment within which the processes will transform the phenomena. They answer the questions, *"Where and when will the processes take place?"* For example, operationally defined conditions orient an employee to apply principles to his or her specific responsibilities and specific purposes.

APPLICATIONS

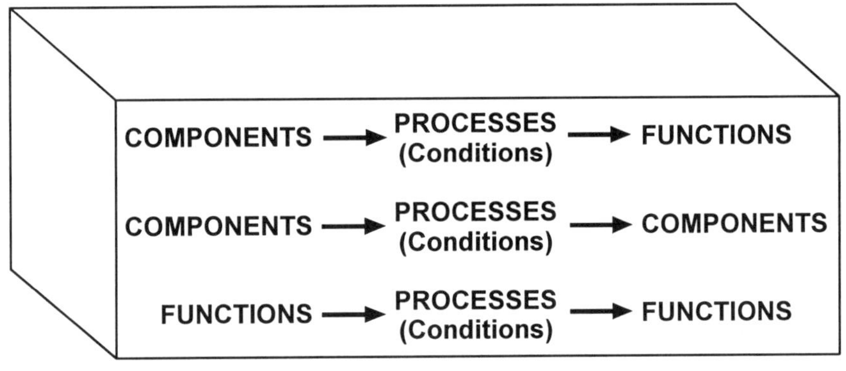

Applications

Objectives are traditionally viewed as achievable operations. We may conceive of objectives as the operations or systems that define phenomenon. Key to defining phenomena are the standards or levels of achievement or excellence that complete our definition of the phenomenon. The standards answer the questions, *"How well must we perform?"* or *"How good must the phenomenon be?"* Standards also serve to recycle feedback to upgrade the system. For example, an employee is empowered by operations to implement his or her responsibilities.

OBJECTIVES

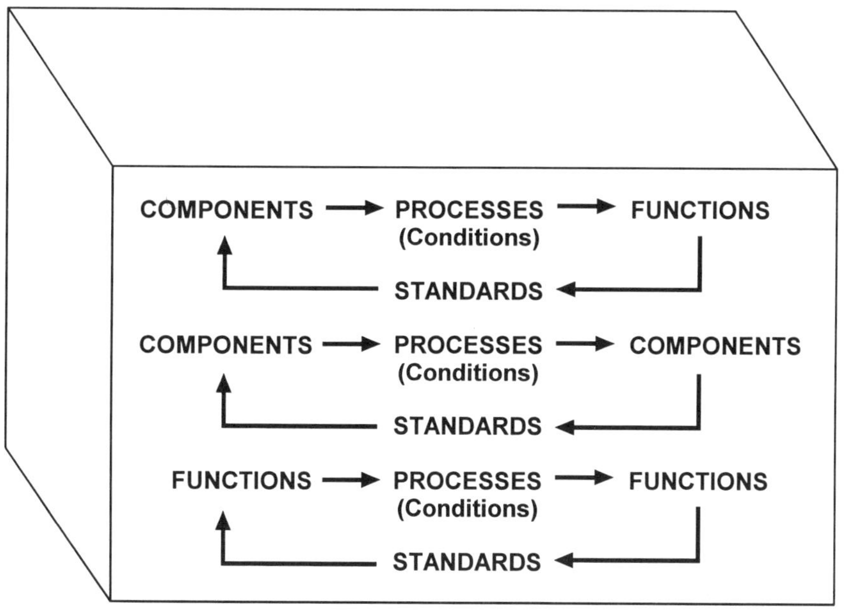

Objectives

To check our own level of information relating, we may plot our daily functioning in our different areas of applications. Here we may employ levels of operations as our indices. We qualify for functional operations if we can define the results outputs of what we are doing; for components, if we can define the resource inputs invested in what we are doing; for processes, if we can define the procedures for transforming our components into functions; for conditions, if we can define the contexts for the processes; for standards, if we can define the levels of achievement to which we aspire.

LEVELS OF OPERATIONS

5	FUNCTIONS
4	COMPONENTS
3	PROCESSES
2	CONDITIONS
1	STANDARDS

Operationalizing Profile

The functions level of operations emphasizes the purposes or outputs of our processing system. They may be products, services or solutions. If we employ the development of our own HCD model as an illustration, then our basic functions are to live, learn and work productively. In this case, we are viewing the people themselves as the products.

FUNCTIONS

- WORKING

- LEARNING

- LIVING

Functions

II. The HCD Ingredients

The components level of operations emphasizes the investments or inputs we invest in our processing system. They may be people, data or things. If we employ the HCD model, then our basic components are physical, emotional and intellectual resources. In this case, we are employing the peoples' resources as the investments.

COMPONENTS

- INTELLECTUAL
- EMOTIONAL
- PHYSICAL

Components

The processes level of operations emphasizes the procedures or methods that transform the components into functions. They are usually processing systems of one kind or another. Again, employing the HCD model yields the basic human processing systems: S–R conditioned responding, S–O–R discrimination learning; S–P–R generative processing. In this case, we are viewing the people's processing systems as the transforming processes.

PROCESSES

- S–P–R PROCESSING

- S–O–R LEARNING

- S–R CONDITIONING

Processes

The conditions level of operations emphasizes the contexts or environments within which the processing systems take place. The conditions are themselves processing systems with functions, components and processes. They determine the functions that drive the processing systems. For example, with the HCD model, the HCD is nested in organizational systems that themselves have market-driven functions inherited from the marketplace. In this case, the HCD system is *"nested"* within an organization capital development system, or OCD.

CONDITIONS

- MARKETPLACE

- ORGANIZATION

- HUMAN

Conditions

The standards level of operations emphasizes the levels of achievement or excellence to which the processing system is dedicated. Again, the standards are themselves processing systems with functions, components and processes. They measure the performance of the system to which they are dedicated. Again, the HCD model generates information standards to measure its performance. In this case, the information capital development, or ICD, system is *"nested"* in the HCD system.

STANDARDS

- HUMAN

- INFORMATION

- MECHANICAL

Standards

We can rate individuals' levels of learning according to their modal levels of functioning. Thus, the individuals are rated at the level that dominates their functioning in all applications. It is noteworthy that individuals functioning modally above minimally effective levels are always defining applications and objectives in their substantive specialties. People functioning below minimally effective levels are never making applications simply because they do not know why or how to do so. If we cannot define applications and objectives, we cannot achieve them. Thus, we cannot be actualized in our intellectual substance.

Levels of Information Relating	Areas of Application				
	Home	School	Work	Org.	Community
5 Standards					
4 Conditions					
3 Processes					
2 Components					
1 Functions					

Modal Learning Profile

The substance of any and all operational information involves the description of its components, functions, processes, conditions and standards. Current dictionaries illustrate a vagueness of understanding for words that attempt to describe information. Words like *"concepts," "principles"* and *"systems"* have been particularly confusing. The pages of this chapter, however, present *"facts," "concepts," "principles," "objectives"* and *"programs"* in terms of the relations of their operations: functions, components, processes, conditions, standards. These definitions allow us to build operational information. This is the generic "content" of all information.

Information Building

Once again, the growthful learner moves developmentally and cumulatively through the levels of informational learning: gathering facts; relating them in concepts; explaining them in principles; employing them in applications; operationalizing them in objectives. Operationalizing information is the precondition for all processing. It is both stimulus input and, in its prime form, output. If we cannot define, then we cannot think! In the final analysis, there is no processing without operations; and ultimately no operations without processing!

The Substantive Perspective

To sum, all processing begins with operational information. Without operational information, we have nothing to process, for processing is the transformation of one level of conceptual content to another more operational level. In this context, there is no *"permanent"* content. All content is merely a transitional product of processing. In short, all processing begins—but does not end—with operational information. The learning of all content is conditional upon the changing requirements of processing!

The Operationalizers

7. Information Representing— The Modelers

Armed with the operational information derived from relating, we can now build upon those operations in modeling. Modeling is simply the ability to develop multidimensional images of operations. We simply cannot process generatively without multidimensional models. While we may have random success with conceptual or operational information, we cannot generate new ideas systematically without modeling. Modeling empowers us to view all dimensions of all of our operations in perspective.

Information Modeling → **Multidimensional Images**

We really cannot process productively without modeling. In other words, modeling enables us to expand our alternatives before narrowing upon our preferred alternative. For example, in *"Workforce XXI,"* we teach the candidates how to transform linear operations into multidimensional models. Modeling is perhaps the most difficult of all HCD skills for most candidates. Until recently, they have only been required to think in linear terms. Only now have they begun to think in terms of two-dimensional matrices. Modeling is the threshold requirement for processing generatively.

Multi-D Images → Processing

Somewhere in the annals of science and engineering the first operational definitions were developed. The scientists needed these operations to define their hypothetical constructs. The engineers required them to achieve their objectives. Scholars such as Mager in education and Gilbert in management made applications utilizing these operational definitions: functions are discharged by components enabled by processes under specifiable conditions and with measurable standards.

OPERATIONS
(Gilbert, 1978; Mager, 1962)

FUNCTIONS

COMPONENTS

PROCESSES

CONDITIONS

STANDARDS

Historical Context

The first systems thinkers such as Taylor transformed these operations into systems, as illustrated below: components inputs are transformed into functions outputs by procedural processes. Basically, the modeler decides *what* it is he or she is attempting to achieve (functions); *who* and *what* must be invested (components); *how* and *why* this can be accomplished (processes); *where* and *when* things will be performed (conditions); *how well* they must be performed (standards).

SYSTEMS MODELING
(Taylor, 1967)

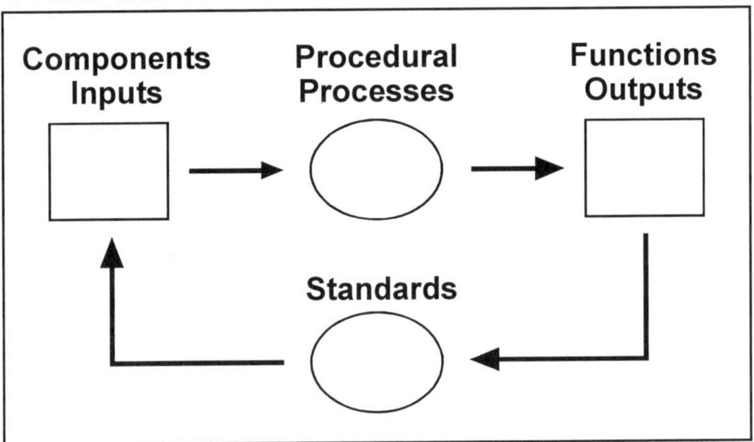

Systems Modeling

These processing systems may be fluidly transformed into multidimensional models as illustrated below. Multidimensional modeling yields the benefits of *"mapping in"* the various interactions. As well, it allows us to build complex schematic images. Most important is the need to define the dimensions of phenomena in a disciplined manner: functions, components, processes, conditions, standards.

MULTIDIMENSIONAL MODELING
(Carkhuff, 1984)

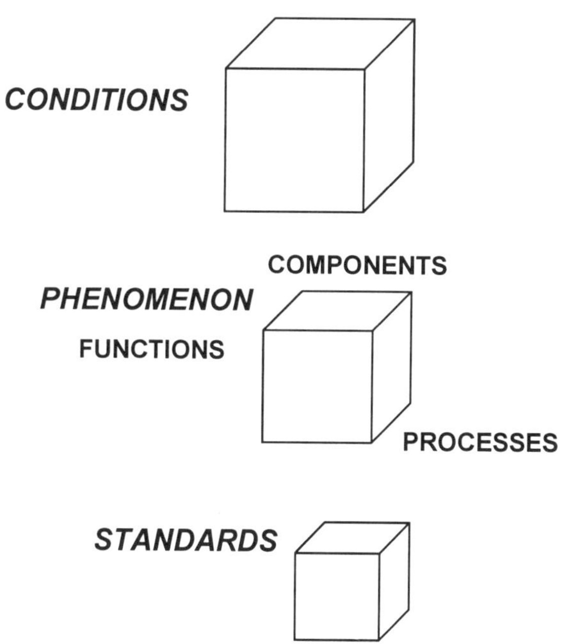

Multidimensional Modeling

We may scale these levels of information representing. At the lowest level, there are only one-dimensional representations. Next there are two-dimensional representations; then three-dimensional; followed by nested dimensionality; and finally, multidimensionality.

LEVELS OF INFORMATION REPRESENTING
(Carkhuff, 1984)

5	MULTI-D
4	NESTED D
3	3D
2	2D
1	1D

Levels of Information Representing

We may illustrate one-dimensional, linear representations in the functions of modeling-building. Simply scale the functions from the highest or superordinate level to the lowest or most subordinate level. For example, we may scale human capital development or HCD functions from basic living tasks such as relating through learning tasks to working tasks. At higher levels, we may add organizing tasks and community or cultural development tasks and other HCD functions.

FUNCTIONS

1D Representations

Similarly, we may illustrate two-dimensional matrices by relating different sets of dimensions. Simply scale the dimensions and interact them. Again, it is imperative to follow the discipline of dedicating components to discharging functions. Thus, for example, the following components may be dedicated to accomplishing HCD functions: physical, emotional and intellectual resource components. At higher levels, we may add social, spiritual and other resource components.

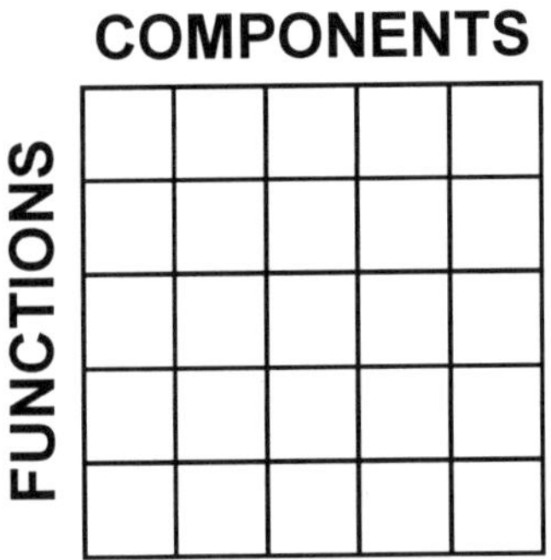

2D Representations

Likewise, we may illustrate three-dimensional models by continuing to relate a third scaled dimension. Again, to be systematic, we must be disciplined in our modeling: functions are discharged by components enabled by processes. Thus, for example, the following processes may enable the resource components to discharge the HCD functions: S-R conditioned responding, S-O-R discriminative learning, S-P-R generative processing. At higher levels, we may add S-OP-R organizational processing and S-PP-R phenomenal processing of any kind.

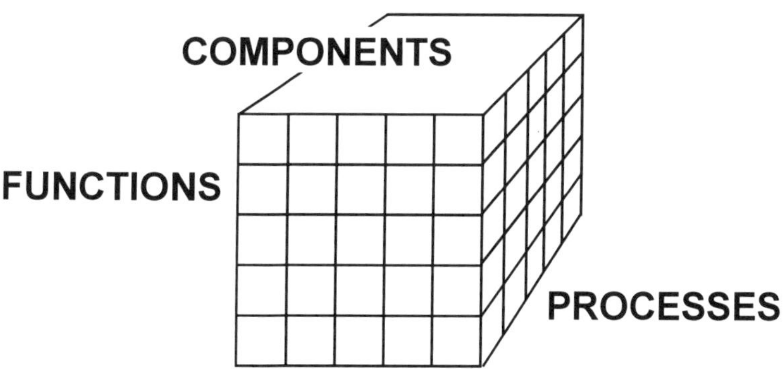

3D Representations

In the same manner, we may illustrate nested modeling by relating to other models. In the illustration, the phenomenon is nested in the conditions of its environment. The conditions are themselves represented by three-dimensional models with their own functions, components and processes. For example, the conditions for the HCD phenomenon may be organizational phenomena. Again, we are disciplined in our modeling: functions are discharged by components enabled by processes under specifiable conditions.

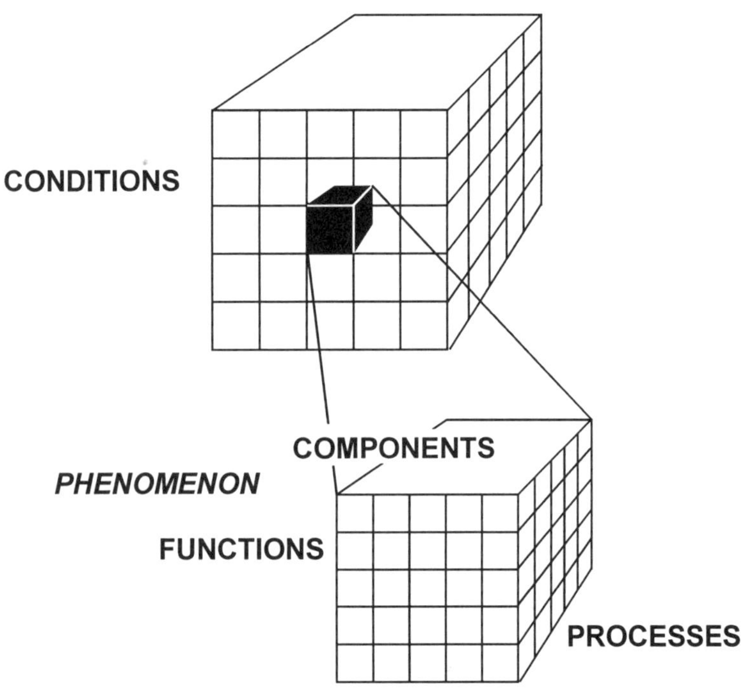

Nested Representations

Finally, we may illustrate multidimensional modeling by continuing to relate to other models. In the illustration, the phenomenon generates standards for its performance. Again, the standards are, themselves, represented by three-dimensional models with their own functions, components and processes. For example, the standards for the HCD phenomenon may be information phenomena. We read our operations systematically: functions are discharged by components enabled by processes under specifiable conditions with measurable standards.

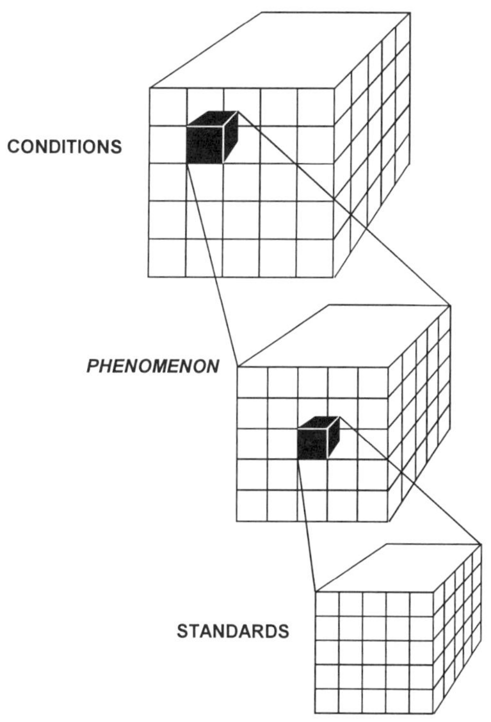

Multidimensional Representations

To check our own level of information representing, we may plot our daily functioning in our different areas of application. We qualify for the 1D level with linear representations of operations such as step-by-step programs; the 2D level with matrices dedicating components to functions; the 3D level with models adding enabling processes; the nested D level with models adding contextual conditions; the multi-D level with models adding standards for performance.

LEVELS OF INFORMATION REPRESENTING
(Carkhuff, 1984)

5	**MULTI-D**
4	**NESTED D**
3	**3D**
2	**2D**
1	**1D**

Levels of Information Representing

For example, we may represent organizational functions linearly as illustrated below. This scale may represent the function of an organizationally driven HCD model, as we will soon see. In other words, HCD resources are dedicated to discharging organizational functions.

ORGANIZATIONAL FUNCTIONS

LEADERSHIP

MARKETING

RESOURCES

TECHNOLOGY

PRODUCTION

Linear Representations

By scaling the resource components dedicated to achieving organizational functions, we may develop a two-dimensional matrix. As may be viewed, the human components are dedicated to the organizational functions.

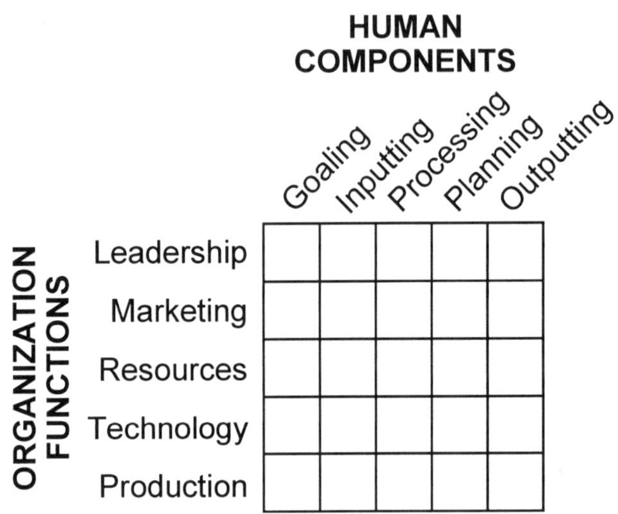

Matrix Representations

By further scaling the processes that enable the human components to discharge organizational functions, we may illustrate a three-dimensional model. As may be viewed, the very information representing skills that we are studying empower the human components to discharge organizational functions.

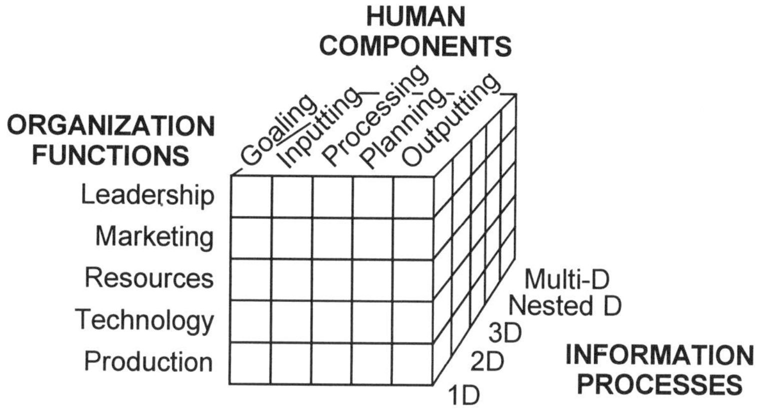

Modeling Representations

By developing further three-dimensional models, we may illustrate the conditions within which the human phenomena are nested. Again, the organizational conditions are themselves three-dimensional models that generate the organizational functions of the human phenomena.

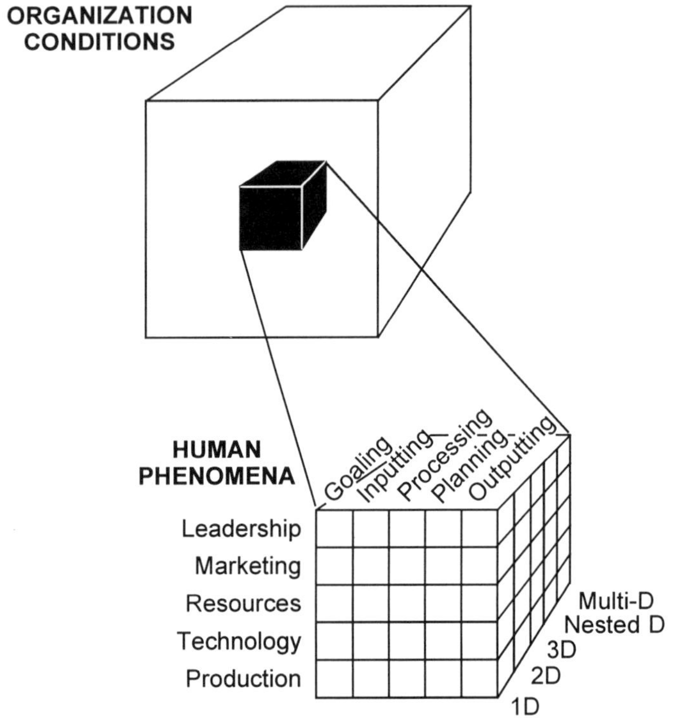

Nested Modeling Representations

Finally, by developing other three-dimensional models, we may illustrate the standards that are generated by the human phenomena. Again, the information standards are themselves three-dimensional models that measure the performance of the human phenomena.

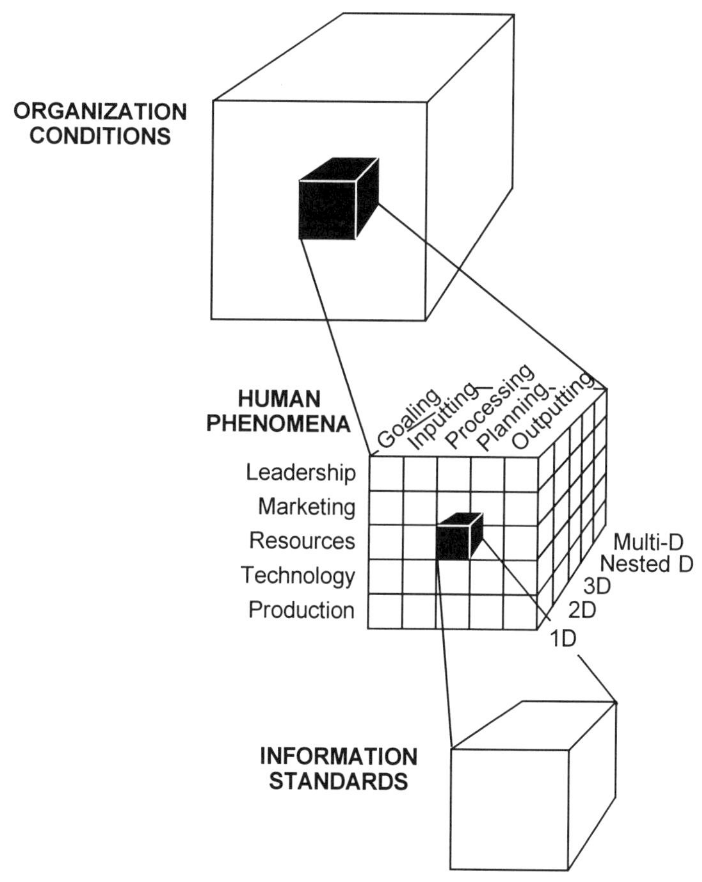

Multidimensional Modeling Representations

II. The HCD Ingredients

We can rate individuals' levels of information representing according to their modal levels of functioning. Thus, the individuals are rated at the level that dominates their functioning at home, school, work, in organizations and in the community. It is important to emphasize that people who are capable of 3D modeling qualify for systematic processing: those who do not, do not! If we cannot model multidimensionally, then we cannot view operations in perspective.

Levels of Information Representing	Areas of Application				
	Home	School	Work	Org.	Community
5 – Multi-D					
4 – Nested D					
3 – 3D					
2 – 2D					
1 – 1D					

Modal Information Representing Profile

If we cannot model multidimensionally, then we cannot view operations in perspective. If we cannot see operations in perspective, then we cannot see alternatives. If we cannot see alternatives, then we cannot process generatively in a systematic manner. Information representing skills are the key to processing of any kind.

Information Representing Skills

Information representing skills, then, are necessary but not sufficient conditions for processing. They are necessary because we cannot see things clearly without them. They are insufficient because we have not yet begun to process. Information representing skills are the basic building blocks of processing because they enable us to expand our options before narrowing them to preferred alternatives.

Information Representing Perspective

To sum, the precondition of all processing is information representing or modeling. Without modeling, our successes in processing are random. With modeling, our successes in processing are systematic. The modeler is the model for the prepared processor!

The Modelers

8. Individual Processing—The Thinkers

The goal of *"Workforce XXI"* is to develop human capital. What makes people *"capital"* is their ability to think. Thinking is the process of transforming the raw data of human experience into productive information. Productive information means that the content is defined in operational terms. Productive information makes the information useful: it can be acted upon. In *"Workforce XXI,"* we build upon the learning of operational content by empowering the candidates to build their own content. This means that the candidates can transform any data inputs into productive information outputs.

Thinking → Productive Ideas

Moreover, we can systematically transform productive information into prime information. Prime information means that
the information is significantly more productive than the original information. In other words, we can intentionally generate
better ways of seeing and doing things. In *"Workforce XXI,"* we
do this by empowering candidates' experience, understanding
their goals, acting upon their programs. Defining their own
goals, the candidates can learn to generate new and more productive responses for any and every function in their lives.

**Productive
Information** → **Prime
Information**

At the most productive levels, we can produce a spiraling flow of prime responses. Each cycle of processing is continuous: the outputs of the first cycle become the inputs of the second cycle and so on. We do not have to accept the status quo in any area. We can go on to generate new and more productive ways of doing things in every area. And, we can do so intentionally and systematically! We can generate our own destinies. Having said this, we truly become *"capital"* for others only when we dedicate ourselves to capital functions outside of our own self-serving boundaries. In other words, we relate to process our worlds—to transform data into information capital, people into human capital, teams into team capital, organizations into organization capital, communities into community capital. As they become empowered with individual thinking skills, the workforce members will discover the productive power of processing: they do not have to accept things as they are; they can employ their brainpower to improve them.

Prime Information → **Spiraling Information**

The majority of the history of humankind is the history of conditioned responding. Basically, conditioned responding or S-R conditioning means that people are systematically *"conditioned"* to make reflex or *"knee-jerk"* type responses to the stimulus conditions that are presented to them. In other words, the stimulus conditions (S) elicit the conditioned response (R)—without the intervention of any human processing or thinking. In fact, S–R conditioned responding does involve anticipatory s–r *"sets,"* or *"chains"* of s–r sequences that are stored and then applied by the human organism. However, even in the most advanced or adaptive form, the conditioned human performer is no more than the accumulation of s–r *sets.* A problem occurs when the requirements of the environment change and the conditioned response is inadequate or dysfunctional.

CONDITIONED RESPONDING
(Skinner, 1938)

$$S \longrightarrow \left(s\text{--}r\text{--}s\text{--}r\text{--}s\text{--}r \right) \longrightarrow R$$

Historical Context

In discriminative learning, the human organism (O) builds up a repertoire or hierarchy of conditioned S–R responses in order to meet the changing conditions of tasks to be performed. This repertoire of responses becomes a reservoir for discriminating stimulus conditions (S) and selecting and emitting appropriate responses (R). In its optimum form, the potential of S–O–R learning is the accumulation of all currently known responses, or the sum of the S–R *sets*. A problem occurs when the requirements of the environment change more rapidly than the responses can be learned. Ultimately, all conditioned responding is dysfunctional or pathological—no matter how extensive the repertoire—because of its inability to respond effectively to the changing conditions of the environment.

DISCRIMINATIVE LEARNING
(Hull, 1951)

$$S \rightarrow \left(\begin{array}{c} O \\ S_n - R_n \\ S... - R... \\ S_1 - R_1 \end{array} \right) \rightarrow R$$

Generative Contributions

In our own work, we have found that when the requirements of the environment change more rapidly than response repertoires can be collected, then generative processing is necessary. Generative processing begins with a repertoire of discriminative learning skills or S–O–R *sets* such as decision-making, problem-solving, or programming. Generative thinking emphasizes processing with these S–O–R *sets*. By utilizing combinations and permutations of S–O–R *sets,* generative processing emphasizes the human processor (P) as the generator of new and more productive responses. At the extreme, the processor can generate responses that the stimulus conditions were not intended to elicit. Insodoing, the processor creates new environmental requirements. In its optimum form, the potential of S–P–R thinking is the product of the S–O–R *sets* (n) to the nth power.

GENERATIVE PROCESSING
(Carkhuff, 1986)

$$P$$

$$S \rightarrow \left(\begin{array}{c} S_n - O_n - R_n \\ S... - O... - R... \\ S_1 - O_1 - R_1 \end{array} \right) \rightarrow R$$

Generative Processing

The generative S–P–R processing model may be viewed in greater detail. Basically, stimulus inputs (S) are processed or transformed into response outputs (R) by the human processors (P). Processing involves exploring experience by analyzing the operational dimensions of the input; understanding goals by synthesizing new and more productive operations; acting upon programs by operationalizing the tasks to be performed. The feedback from the new response is recycled as new input to stimulate more extensive exploring, more accurate understanding and more productive action.

GENERATIVE PROCESSING MODEL
(Carkhuff, 1992)

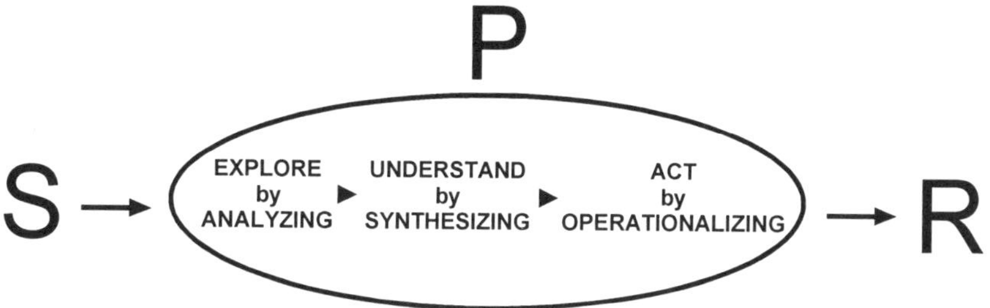

Generative Processing Model

We may scale these levels of thinking. At the lowest level, there is no preparation for thinking. At the next level, the processor prepares by defining his or her goals for thinking. The processor enters the thinking process at level 3 by exploring his or her experience; and continues by understanding new goals in relation to this experience; and culminates processing by acting upon programs to achieve the goals.

LEVELS OF THINKING
(Carkhuff, 1992)

5	**ACTING**
4	**UNDERSTANDING**
3	**EXPLORING**
2	**GOALING**
1	**NON-PREPARATION**

Levels of Thinking

The level of non-preparation simply means that individuals never engage in thinking. At a minimum, this means they never define their goals for thinking. While they may have learned various levels of content, they do not process this content. In other words—without thinking—these learners are consumers of content rather than processors or producers of content. The Information Age now requires processors!

Non-Preparation Level

At the next level, or first phase of processing, the individual processors define the goals or intentions of processing. The requirements for goaling are information representing. The goalers must represent the informational operations multidimensionally in order to process generatively. That way they can *"map-in"* to a perspective of where they are and where they are going.

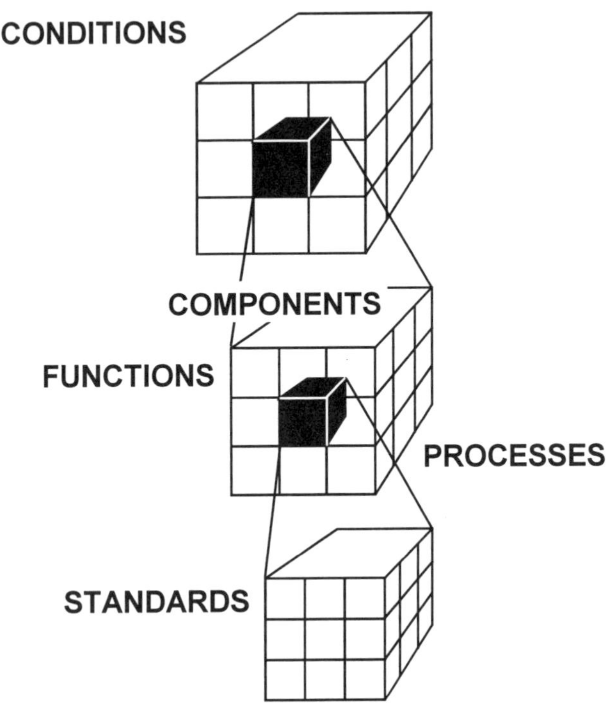

Goaling Level

At the next level, in the second phase of processing, the individual processors explore their experience by analyzing its operations. In the systems representation below, components inputs are transformed into functions outputs by procedural processes. The functions tell us *what* we are doing; the components, *who* and *what* we are investing; the processes, *how* and *why* the components are transformed into functions; the conditions, *where* and *when*; the standards, *how well*.

Contextual Conditions

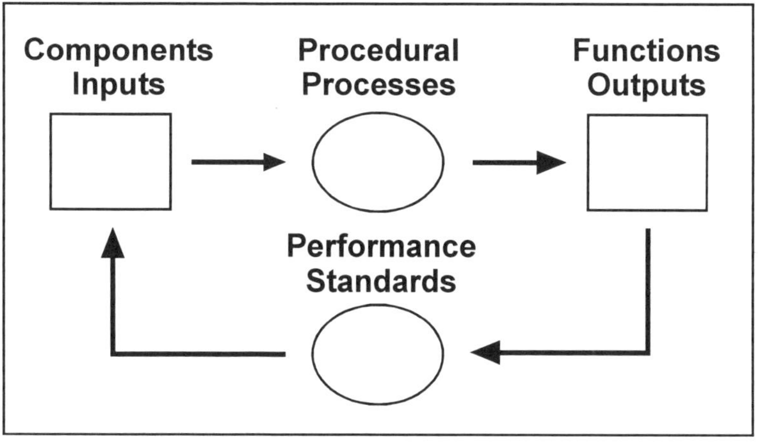

Exploring Level

The key to analyzing operations is analyzing standards. The standards measure *how well* we have achieved our functions outputs. They also measure the cost of components inputs. In other words, they yield a productivity equation comparing the benefits (outputs) with the costs (inputs). *The standards tell us whether we are doing the things right.*

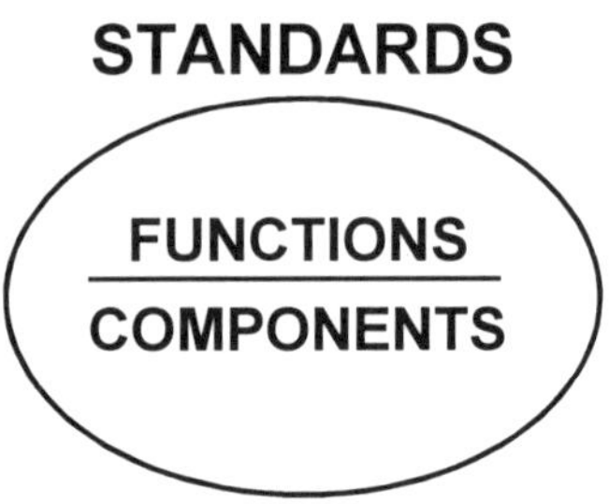

Analyzing Operations

At the next level, in the third phase of processing, the individual processors understand their experience by synthesizing new operations. Again, the systems representation requires increasingly productive standards. In other words, the value of the outputs (benefits) is increasingly greater than the value of the inputs (costs).

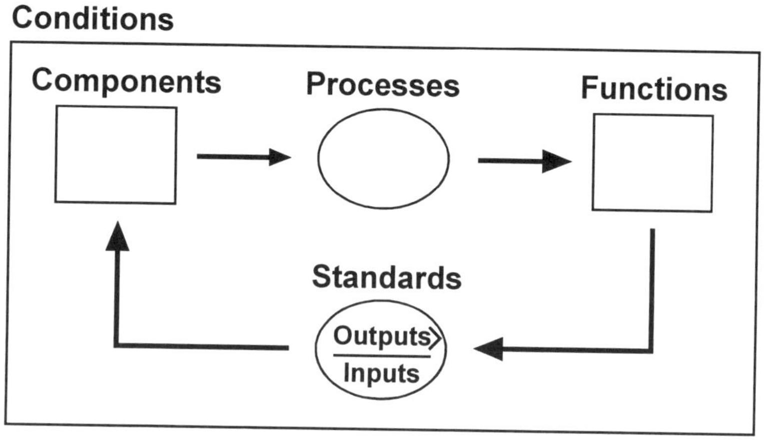

Conditions

Components → **Processes** → **Functions**

Standards

$$\frac{\text{Outputs}}{\text{Inputs}}$$

Understanding Level

The key to synthesizing operations is expanding operations. In the systems representations below, the systems options are expanded by the conditions from which the systems were derived. The conditions not only tell us *where* and *when* the systems apply but also *why* the systems apply. The conditions tell us whether we are doing the right things.

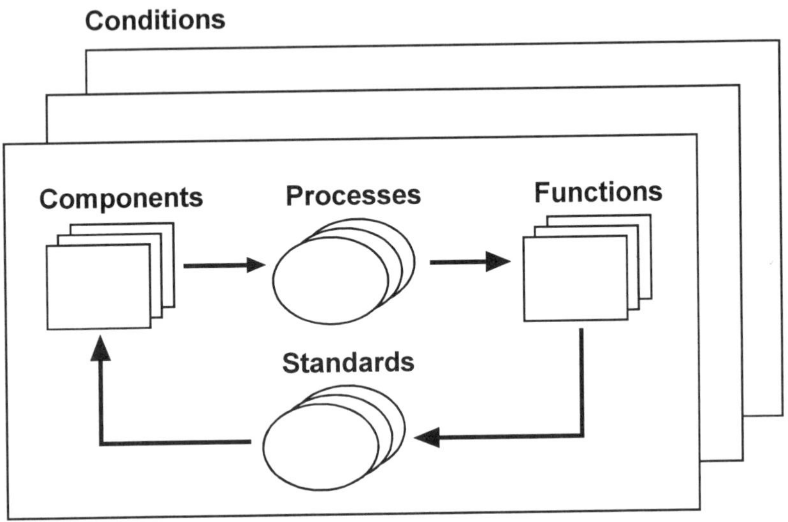

Expanding Operations

Still within synthesizing, the individual processors understand their experience by narrowing from the expanded operations. Using their values, derived from goaling, the operations are narrowed to those meeting the values at the highest levels. We label these *prime operations*. They tell us the best processes for transforming components into functions with the highest standards.

PRIME CONDITIONS

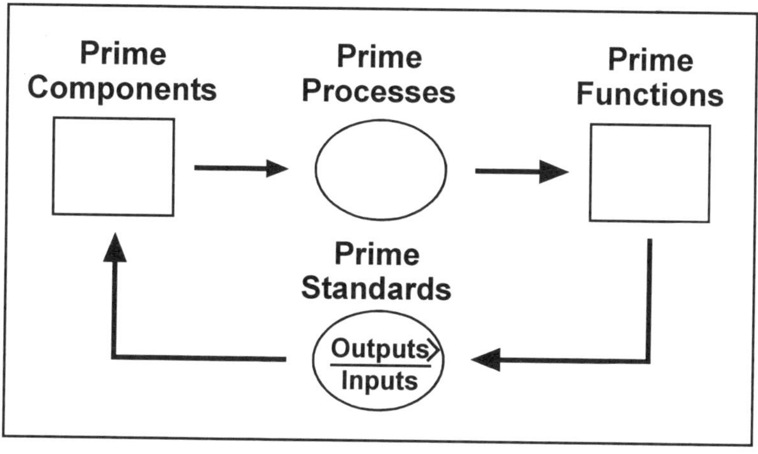

Synthesizing Operations

At the last level, in the final phase of processing, the individual processors act upon their experience by operationalizing their new objectives and programs. Operationalizing our objectives and programs tells us how to achieve our new prime operations: functions, components, processes.

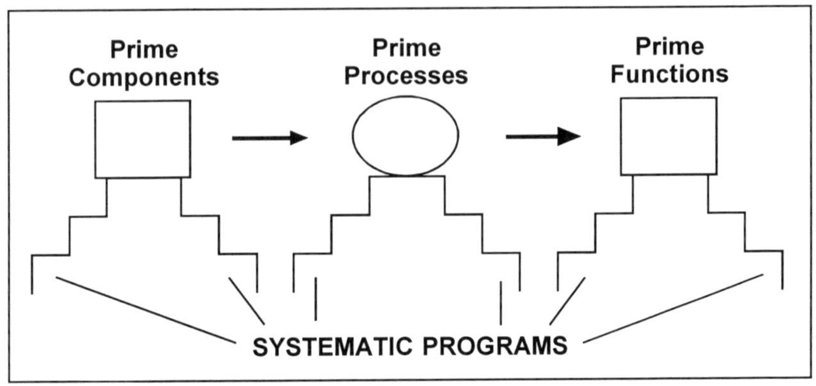

Acting Level

Operationalizing recycles the new operations: functions, components, processes, conditions, standards. Operationalizing also recycles the new systems: programs, steps, sub-steps.

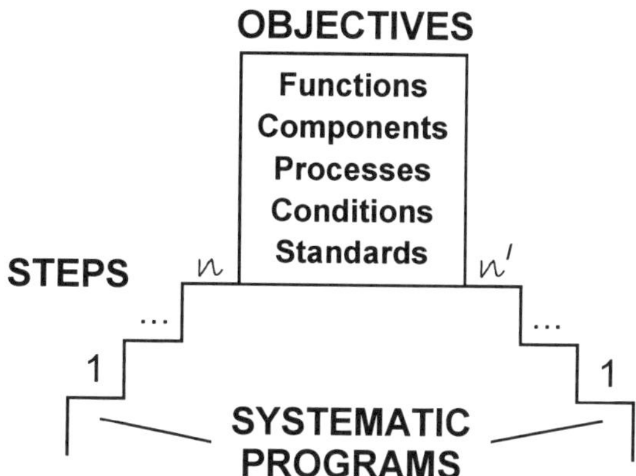

Operationalizing Objectives

Although we have not had systematic training in these thinking skills, we may, nevertheless, wish to check out our own level of thinking by plotting our daily functioning in different areas of application. To qualify, we must have engaged in at least one thinking activity in at least one application area each day: preparing by defining goals for thinking; exploring where we are with our experience; understanding where we want or need to be with our experience; acting to get there. These stringent thinking requirements reflect thinking as a way of life.

LEVELS OF THINKING

5   ACTING

4   UNDERSTANDING

3   EXPLORING

2   GOALING

1   NON-PREPARATION

Thinking Profile

At the level of goaling for processing, we may begin with our image of the goal of processing. The better developed this image, the more productive will be our processing. In the case of HCD, we actually began with a well-developed image of the goal of processing: to develop a comprehensive model for HCD. We may define this HCD model operationally: living, learning and working functions are discharged by physical, emotional and intellectual resource components enabled by S–R conditioned responding and S–O–R discriminative learning systems.

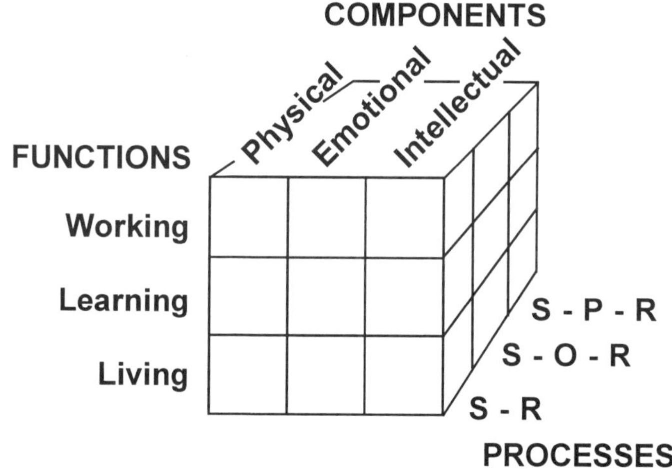

Goaling

At the exploring level of processing, we analyze our goaling image to determine its adequacy for processing purposes. We do this by comparing our outputs (functions) with our inputs (components). This comparison tells us whether we are doing things *right* or correctly In the case of HCD modeling, our standards compare our levels of achievement of living, learning and working functions with our levels of investment of physical, emotional and intellectual resources. If we are unsatisfied with the productivity of this feedback, we continue to the next level of processing.

Exploring

At the understanding level of processing, we expand new images of the systems. First, we expand not only within but between and among the systems. This increases our images of alternative systems. In the case of HCD modeling, we expand alternative HCD systems as derived from higher-order organizational systems.

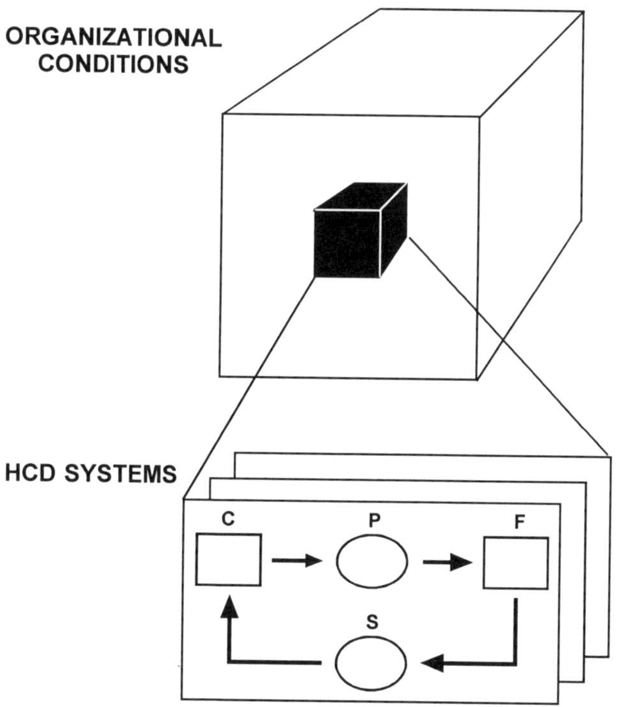

Understanding

Still at the understanding level of processing, we narrow our alternative images to a preferred image. We do this by returning to the values imbedded in our original goal. In the case of HCD, our goal was to develop a comprehensive model for HCD. As may be noted, our functions were expanded to incorporate organization functions; our components were expanded to include information relating and individual processing; our processes were expanded to include S–P–R generative processing systems. We may define this HCD model operationally: living, learning and working functions are discharged by physical, emotional and intellectual resource components enabled by S–P–R-driven processing systems.

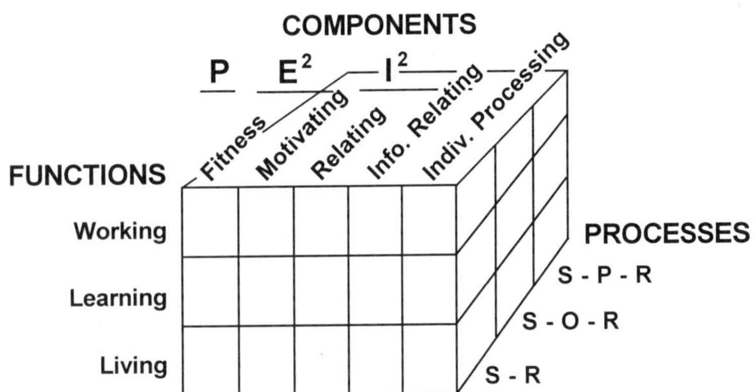

Synthesizing

Finally, we act to operationalize our new synthesized image. We do this by operationally defining our new objectives and programmatically planning and implementing steps to achieve these objectives. In the case of HCD, we operationally define objectives for all the cells of our model and develop systematic programs to achieve these objectives: beginning with living functions discharged by physical components enabled by S-R conditioning; culminating with organization functions discharged by individual processing enabled by S-OP-R organizational processing.

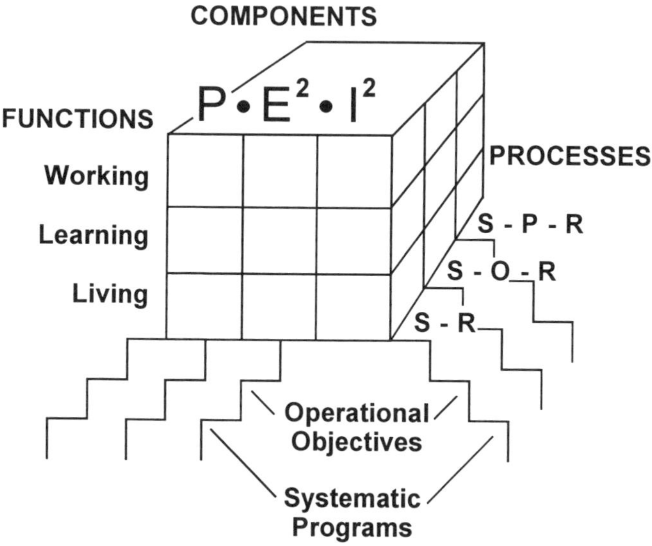

Acting

II. The HCD Ingredients

Here, too, we may rate individuals modally, across their areas of functioning. People who are functioning at modally high levels are always processing content or thinking. People functioning at modally low levels are never processing content—and, thus, never thinking. We are fully alive only if we are thinking fully. We can only approach actualizing our human potential with an effective thinking system.

Levels of Individual Thinking	Areas of Application				
	Home	School	Work	Org.	Community
5 Acting					
4 Understanding					
3 Exploring					
2 Goaling					
1 Non-Preparation					

Modal Thinking Profile

Thinking emphasizes a series of phases. Each phase requires the application of specific thinking skills: exploring experience, understanding goals, acting upon programs. If we want to improve the products of our thinking we must improve our thinking skills. We cannot *"tap"* the awesome power of the human intellect if we do not learn the skills of thinking.

Individual Thinking Skills

Once again, the growthful thinker moves developmentally and cumulatively through the levels of thinking: preparing, exploring, understanding, acting. Individual thinking is the precondition for interpersonal processing. It generates the individual response outputs that serve as stimulus inputs for interpersonal processing. If we cannot think individually, then we cannot process interpersonally. At the highest levels, there is no truly generative interpersonal processing without individual thinking; and no truly generative individual thinking without interpersonal processing!

Thinking Perspective

To sum, thinking is a process that generates new content. Insodoing, thinking accelerates the evolution of ideas. We do not have to wait for the painfully slow gains of evolutionary change. By processing, we can skim across generations of experiential learning and create entirely new stimulus environments. In short, processing is the vehicle of growth. It begins with individual thinking. It moves transitionally through interpersonal processing. It culminates in interdependent processing.

The Thinkers

9. Interpersonal Processing— The Shared Processors

Interpersonal processing is shared processing. We used to say, *"What one can do, a group can do better."* Put another, more conservative way, *"Whatever we can do individually, we can do better with groups."* It all depends upon the skills we employ in shared processing. When the processors share their images, we get one level of benefits. When they merge their images, we get a whole new level of benefits.

Interpersonal Processing → **Better Ideas**

In preparation for *"Workforce XXI,"* we designed and implemented interpersonal processing systems in both private and public sectors. We called these *"Get, Give, Merge and Go"* systems. Basically, people working on the same project got together to process interpersonally as follows:

- *"Getting"* others' images of objectives;
- *"Giving"* one's own image of objectives;
- *"Merging"* images of objectives;
- *"Going"* on to implement the merged image.

By sharing and negotiating merged images of the objectives, the candidates were implementing the basic goal of interpersonal processing: mutual processing for mutual benefit. In other words, they were creating *"Win-Win"* outcomes.

Shared Processing → Shared Benefits

The historical context for interpersonal processing is found in interpersonal facilitating: we attend, respond, personalize and initiate in order to facilitate another's involvement, exploration, understanding and acting. In other words, we respond to facilitate the other's ability to formulate a response. It is critical to emphasize the principle of interpersonal facilitation: *relating is the precondition of all learning.* We relate to phenomena as well as people by using our interpersonal facilitation skills.

INTERPERSONAL FACILITATING
(Carkhuff, 1972)

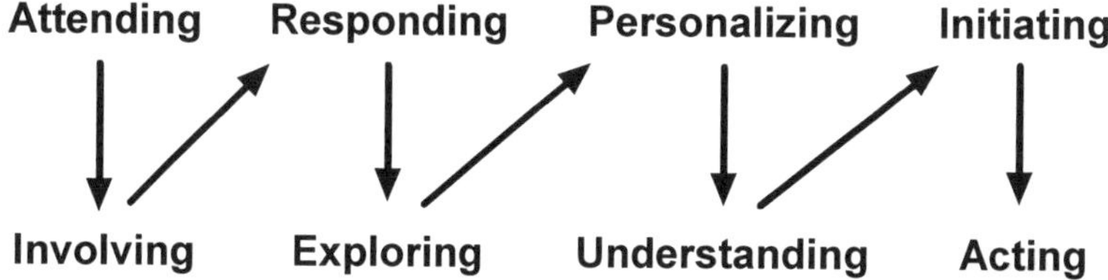

Historical Context

II. The HCD Ingredients

We utilize precisely the same skills in interpersonal processing that we used in interpersonal relating. But we dedicate them to a different purpose: generating new and better images of things. Accordingly, we use the skills in a different manner:

- Responding skills are dedicated to receiving the images of operations.
- Initiating skills are dedicated to sharing our own images of operations.
- Personalizing skills are dedicated to negotiating merged images of operations.

Interpersonal Skills

Interpersonal processing begins with responding. We respond to others' frames of reference in order to *"get"* their images of responses. Their images include any phenomena relevant to the purposes of processing. They might be images of goals or objectives, decisions or problems, requirements or values. In other words, we respond to *get* others' images of the products or outputs of their processing.

INTERPERSONAL RESPONDING
(Carkhuff, 1969)

Getting by Responding

After responding to *get* the images of others, we initiate to *"give"* our own images. Again, we share our images of relevant phenomena. In other words, each individual processes his or her own unique response before sharing an image of that response with others. Clearly, in order to generate our responses, we must relate to ourselves by exploring, understanding and acting.

INTERPERSONAL INITIATING
(Carkhuff, 1972)

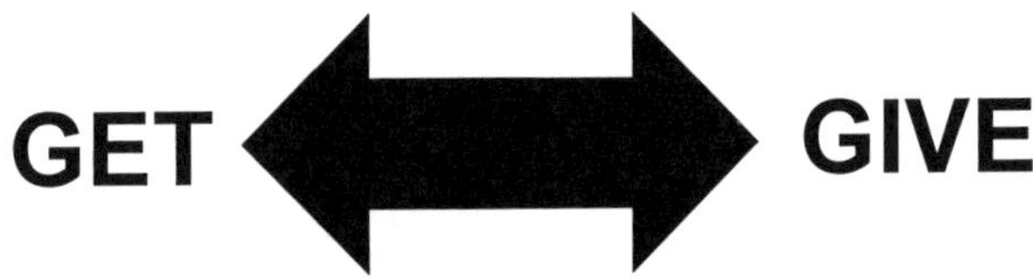

Giving by Initiating

The next stage involves elevating the response by *"merging"* images of responses. The images are *"merged"* by integrating the parts of available responses into a *"best"* response. The processing for *merging* is decision-making based upon shared and operational values and requirements. In this paradigm, individuals *get* and *give* their images before *merging* images.

INTERPERSONAL DECISION-MAKING
(Carkhuff, 1974)

Merging by Decision-Making

The original paradigm was *"Get, Give, Merge and Go."* After processing the merged image, the processors would *"go"* on to plan the achievement of that image. They would plan their program in the same manner that they had processed the image: by *getting, giving* and *merging* images of the goals and the systems and programs needed to achieve the goals.

INTERPERSONAL PLANNING
(Carkhuff, 1984)

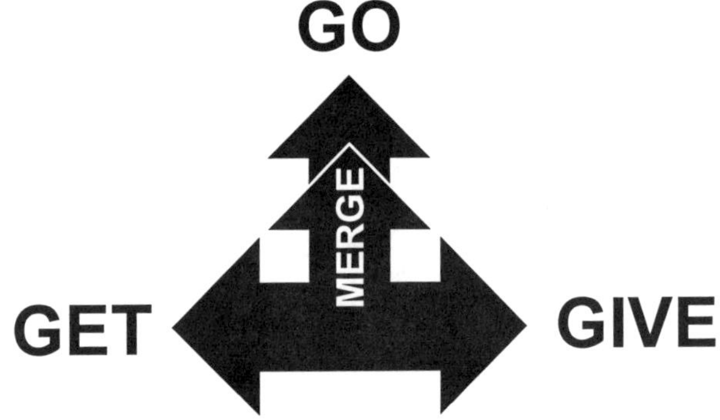

Going on to Planning

In the interpersonal processing paradigm, the processors share and merge images before planning:

- Getting others' images;
- Giving one's own images;
- Merging images;
- Going on to plan to achieve images.

Again, we labeled this interpersonal processing paradigm, *Get, Give, Merge and Go.*

LEVELS OF INTERPERSONAL PROCESSING
(Carkhuff, 1984)

5	GOING
4	MERGING
3	GIVING
2	GETTING
1	NON-PREPARATION

Levels of Interpersonal Processing

The level of non-preparation simply means that individuals never engage in interpersonal processing. This means that they never receive the images of others. They may even have developed their own images through individual processing. However, they never share this image with others. In other words, they may be independent thinkers in a time requiring interpersonal processors.

Non-Preparation Level

At the level of getting images, this means employing responding skills to elicit operational images: functions discharged by components enabled by processes. The same responding skills may be employed to get multiple images from different people.

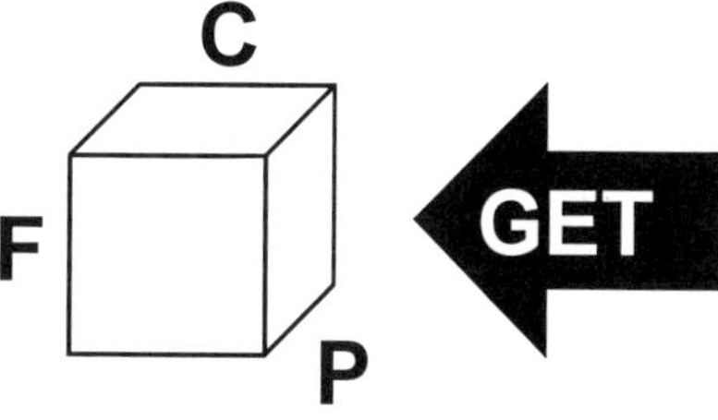

Level of Getting Images

At the level of giving images, this means employing initiating skills to offer operational images: functions, components, processes. These images should be prime images because we have had the opportunity to incorporate the earlier images we have received.

Level of Giving Images

At the level of merging images, this means employing negotiating and decision-making skills to personalize merged images with new functions, components and processes. These images should be super-prime images because we have had the opportunity to incorporate the best features of all other images.

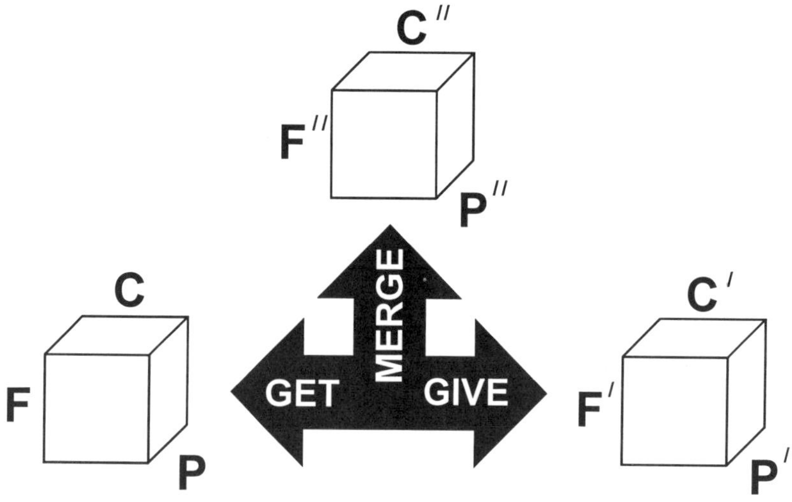

Level of Merging Images

At the level of going on to plan images, this means operationalizing and program development skills to insure success in achieving the personalized merged image. We have completed interpersonal processing: getting, giving, merging, going. We have defined images superior to those with which we began.

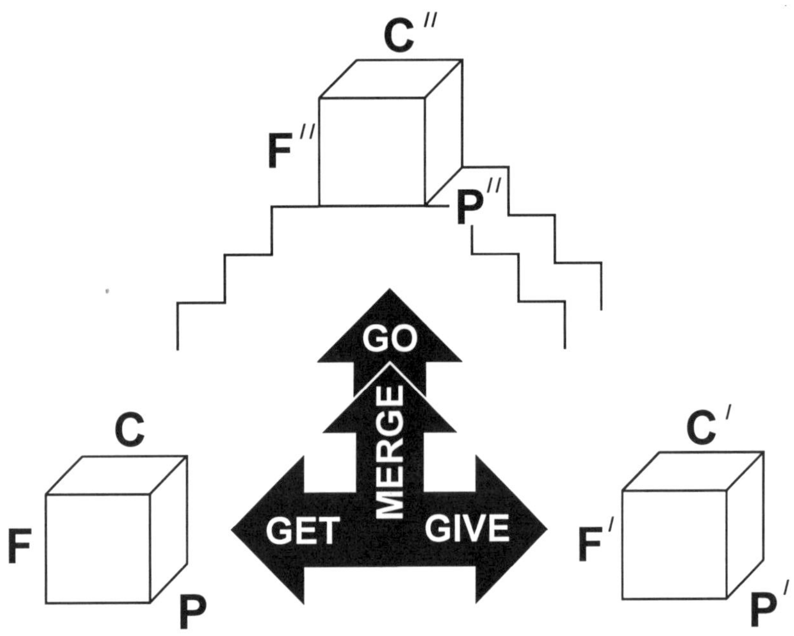

Level of Going on to Plan

To check out our own level of interpersonal processing, we may plot our daily functioning in different areas of applications. To qualify, we must have processed interpersonally by *Get, Give, Merge and Go.*

LEVELS OF INTERPERSONAL PROCESSING

5	GOING ON TO PLAN
4	MERGING IMAGES
3	GIVING IMAGES
2	GETTING IMAGES
1	NON-PREPARATION

Interpersonal Processing Profile

For example, at the level of getting images, we get others' images by responding to their experience. In the case of HCD, we may get early images of the HCD model: living, learning and working functions discharged by physical, emotional and intellectual components enabled by S–R, S–O–R and S–P–R processes.

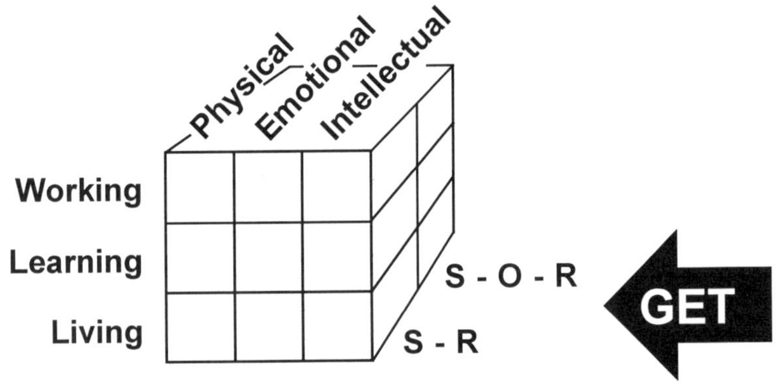

Getting Images

At the level of giving images, we give our images by initiating from our experience. In the case of HCD, we may give advanced images of the HCD model: adding emotional and intellectual components and S–P–R generative processing systems.

Giving Images

II. The HCD Ingredients

At the level of merging images, we merge images by negotiating from a mutual frame of reference. In the case of HCD, we merged prime images of the HCD model: adding mission and phenomenal processing systems. Our merged image is a whole new image of HCD: $P \bullet E^2 \bullet I^3$. We may define this improved image of HCD operationally: systems-driven organizational functions are discharged by intellectual resource-driven components enabled by S–P–R-driven processing systems.

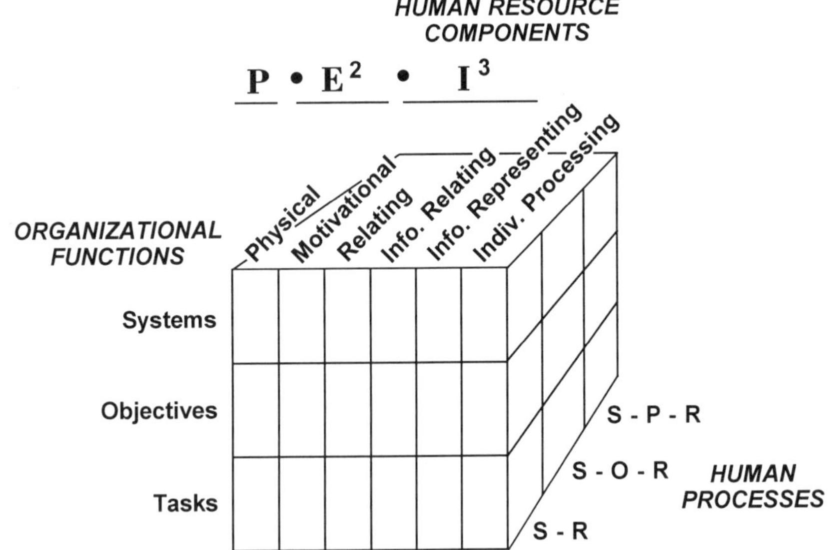

Merging Images

At the level of going on to plan, we define our objectives operationally and develop and implement our programs systematically to achieve these objectives. The objectives range all of the way to the highest-order cell: mission functions are discharged by interdependent processing components enabled by S–O–R phenomenal processing systems.

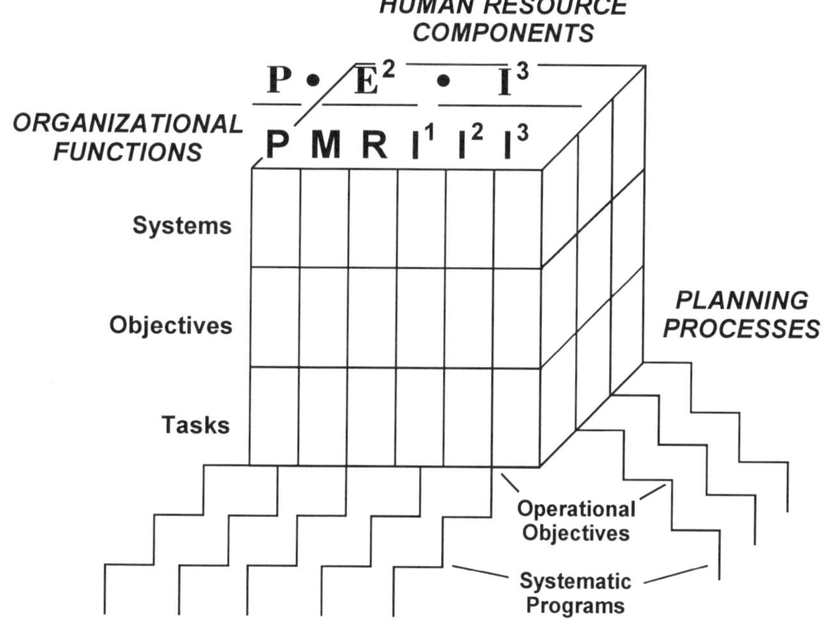

Going on to Planning

Again, we may rate people on their modal levels of functioning across areas. People who are functioning at modally high levels are disposed to sharing and negotiating. People who are functioning at modally low levels are never disposed to sharing. Consequently, the sharers incorporate the ideas of others while the non-sharers do not.

Levels of Interpersonal Processing	**Areas of Application**				
	Home	School	Work	Org.	Community
5 Going					
4 Merging					
3 Giving					
2 Getting					
1 Non- Preparation					

Modal Interpersonal Processing Profile

Interpersonal processing emphasizes shared processing. Sometimes this shared processing precedes individual processing. Most times, it is used most productively after individual processing. The critical threshold is sharing. People who share in processing grow. People who do not share in processing do not grow.

Interpersonal Processing Skills

Once again, growthful people move developmentally and cumulatively within interpersonal processing: getting, giving, merging, going. They also move developmentally and cumulatively among processing systems: individually, interpersonally, interdependently. It remains for us to prepare for interdependent processing based upon both individual and interpersonal processing.

Interpersonal Processing
Perspective

To sum, interpersonal processing is a transitional process that generates new images of phenomena. We ante up to interpersonal processing with the images generated by individual processing. We culminate interpersonal processing with the images generated by interdependent processing. The shared processors are preparing to achieve their full humanity by learning to process interdependently with all people and phenomena.

The Shared Processors

10. Interdependent Processing— The Actualizers

Interdependent processing is the culminating skill of HCD. Interdependent processing is defined as *"mutual processing for mutual benefit."* In one respect, interdependent processing builds upon all other HCD skills: they are necessary but not sufficient conditions of HCD. In another respect, interdependent processing *"dwarfs"* the contributions of all other HCD skills: even individual thinking and interpersonal processing are merely preconditions of interdependent processing. That is because interdependent thinking is, at least in part, a process of relating individual and interpersonal processing. It is also, in part, processing with other phenomena such as organizations. We become *"one"* with the phenomena and process virtually as if we were them. In *"Workforce XXI,"* our HCD candidates soon discover the exhilaration of *"breakthrough"* thinking generated by interdependent processing.

Interdependent Processing → *"Breakthrough"* **Ideas**

The interpersonal processing system led directly to the interdependent processing system. Indeed, the latter system often began where the former system left off—with the merged image of the objective. In these instances, the interdependent processing system utilized the merged objective as stimulus input. In other words, the interpersonal processing system was based upon sharing and merging the products of individual processing. Now, the interdependent processing system was based upon processing this merged image—interdependently! We called this interdependent processing system, *Get, Give, Merge and Grow*. The emphasis was upon *"grow"*—the generating of new images interdependently.

Again, growing focused upon processing virtually with the phenomena. The workforce members will realize the highly leveraged power of interdependent processing to change themselves and their worlds. In other words, they will create *"Grow-Grow"* outcomes.

Mutual Processing → **Generative Processing**

The historical antecedents of interdependent processing lie in individual processing. In individual processing, we process the stimuli into responses:

- Exploring by analyzing operations;

- Understanding by synthesizing new operations;

- Acting by operationalizing new objectives and programs.

Individual processing serves to generate new images of phenomena or stimuli.

INDIVIDUAL PROCESSING
(Carkhuff, 1982)

Individual Processing

In turn, interpersonal processing builds upon the images generated by individual processing:

- Getting others' images of responses (R_1) generated by exploring (E), understanding (U), and acting (A);
- Giving our own images of responses (R_2) generated by E, U, A;
- Merging images of responses (R_3) by negotiating.

As may be noted, we develop three generations of responses (R_1, R_2, R_3) to the same initial stimuli (S_1) in interpersonal processing.

INTERPERSONAL PROCESSING
(Carkhuff, 1984)

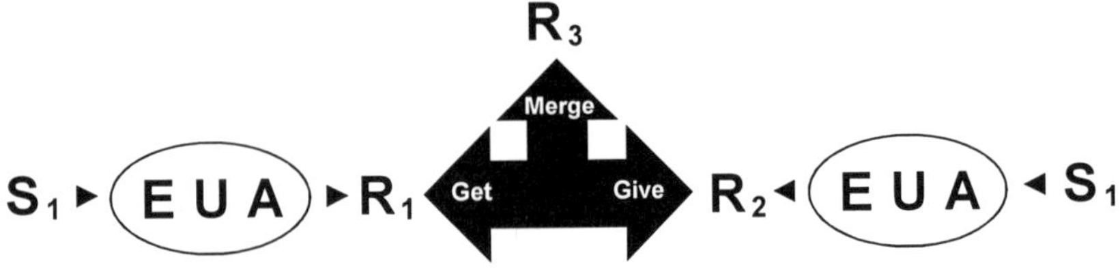

Interpersonal Processing

Finally, we *"grow"* a fourth generation of responses (R_4) by mutually processing the merged response (R_3) as stimulus input. This means getting, giving, merging and growing (GGMG) the new responses:

- GGMG exploring responses;
- GGMG understanding new responses;
- GGMG acting upon new responses.

Again, we grow new generations of responses by mutual processing for mutual benefit.

INTERDEPENDENT PROCESSING
(Carkhuff, 1992)

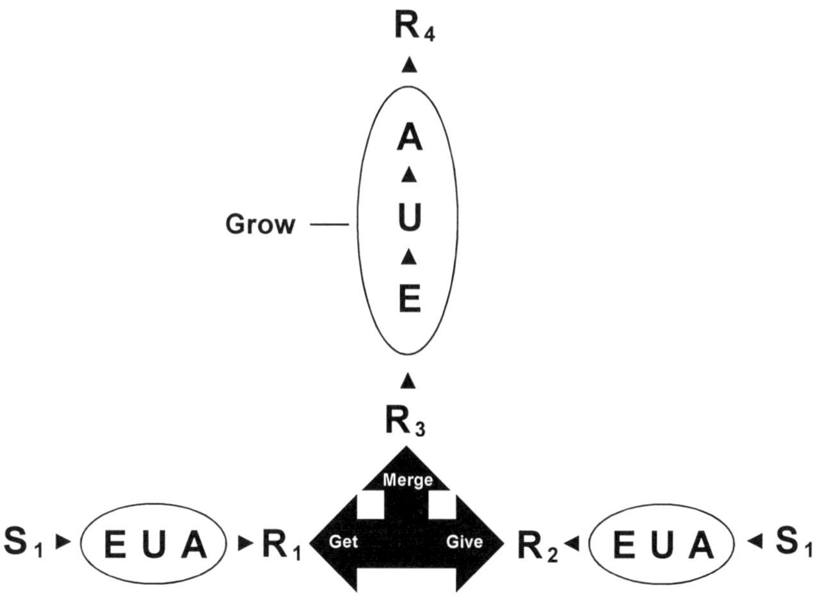

Interdependent processing may be viewed in sharp relief in the matrix for interdependent processing systems. As may be noted below, the interdependent processors implement stages of processing: getting, giving, merging, growing. They do so through all of the phases of processing: goaling, exploring, understanding, acting.

INTERDEPENDENT PROCESSING
(Carkhuff, 1992)

STAGES

PHASES	GET	GIVE	MERGE	GROW
ACTING				
UNDERSTANDING				
EXPLORING				
GOALING				

Interdependent Processing

Interdependent phenomenal processing grows out of applying our individual and interpersonal processing systems to phenomenal processing systems. In the course of processing, we will internalize the processing experience of the phenomena themselves. In the illustration below, we process virtually to generate new capital development functions:

- MCD—Marketplace Capital Development,
- OCD—Organizational Capital Development,
- HCD—Human Capital Development,
- ICD—Information Capital Development,
- mCD—Mechanical Capital Development.

Operationally, this means that new capital development functions are discharged by processing interdependent or I^5 components.

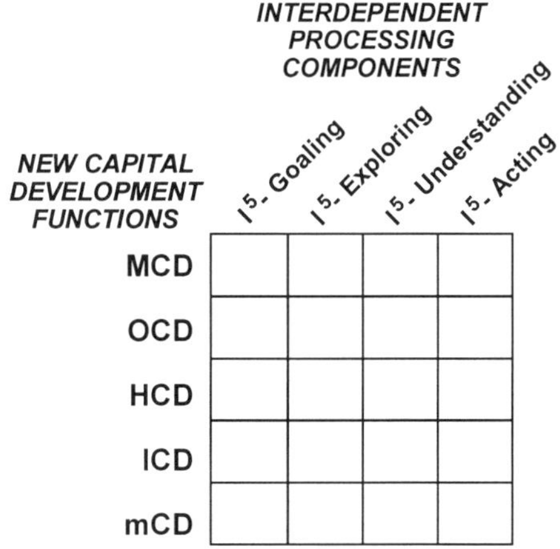

Interdependent Phenomenal Processing

In the interdependent processing paradigm, the processors processed each stage interdependently:

Get, Give, Merge and Grow Goaling

Get, Give, Merge and Grow Exploring

Get, Give, Merge and Grow Understanding

Get, Give, Merge and Grow Acting

Again, we labeled this interdependent processing paradigm *Get, Give, Merge and Grow* because it generated responses that were elevated exponentially over the individual and interpersonal responses.

LEVELS OF INTERDEPENDENT PROCESSING
(Carkhuff, 1992)

5   INTERDEPENDENT ACTING

4   INTERDEPENDENT UNDERSTANDING

3   INTERDEPENDENT EXPLORING

2   INTERDEPENDENT GOALING

1   NON-PREPARATION

Levels of Interdependent Processing

Thus, for example, we may goal OCD tasks by *Getting, Giving, Merging and Growing* as illustrated below: the organizational processing tasks are discharged by goaling components enabled by GGMG processes.

<table>
<tr><td>TASKS ▶</td><td>GET</td><td>GIVE</td><td>MERGE</td><td>GROW</td><td>▶ GOAL TASKS</td></tr>
</table>

GGMG—Goaling Tasks

Similarly, we may explore OCD tasks by GGMG as illustrated below: the organizational tasks are discharged by exploring components enabled by GGMG processes.

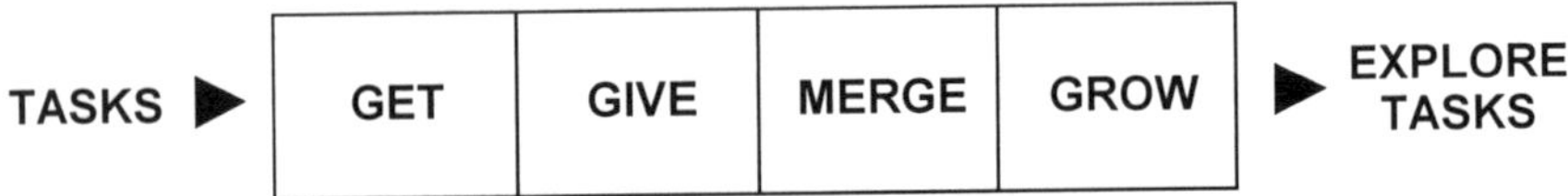

GGMG—Exploring Tasks

Likewise, we may understand OCD tasks by GGMG as illustrated below: the organizational tasks are discharged by understanding components enabled by GGMG processes.

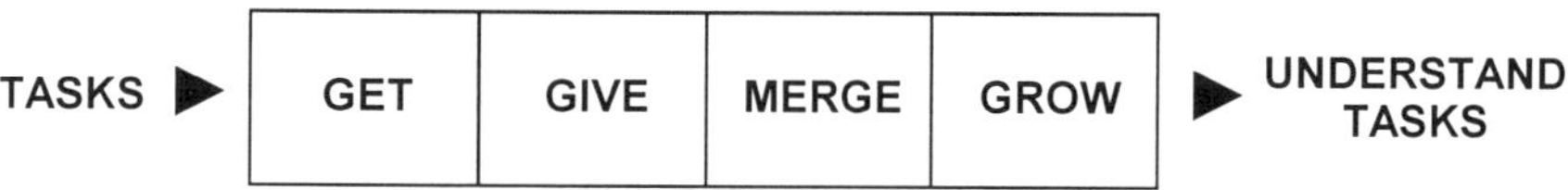

GGMG—Understanding Tasks

Finally, we may act upon OCD tasks by GGMG as illustrated below: the organizational tasks are discharged by acting components enabled by GGMG processes.

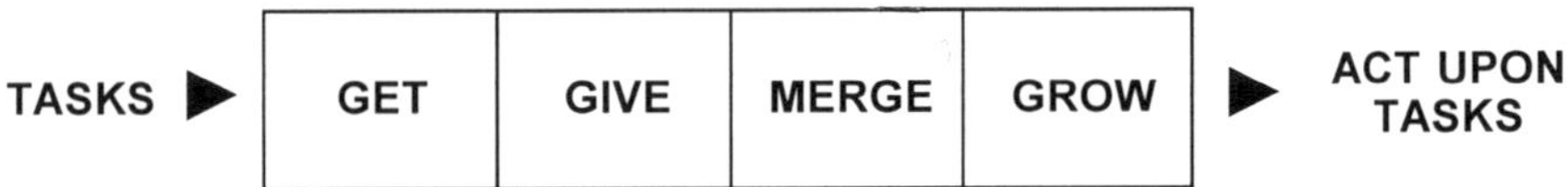

GGMG—Acting upon Tasks

There are other dimensions of interdependent processing. They focus upon the whole phenomena with which we are processing. In the illustration below, we have introduced comprehensive OCD functions: mission, organizational architecture, systems, objectives, tasks. We have already simulated the interdependent processing of tasks on the organizational dimension. We may now simulate the interdependent processing of the remaining organizational dimensions.

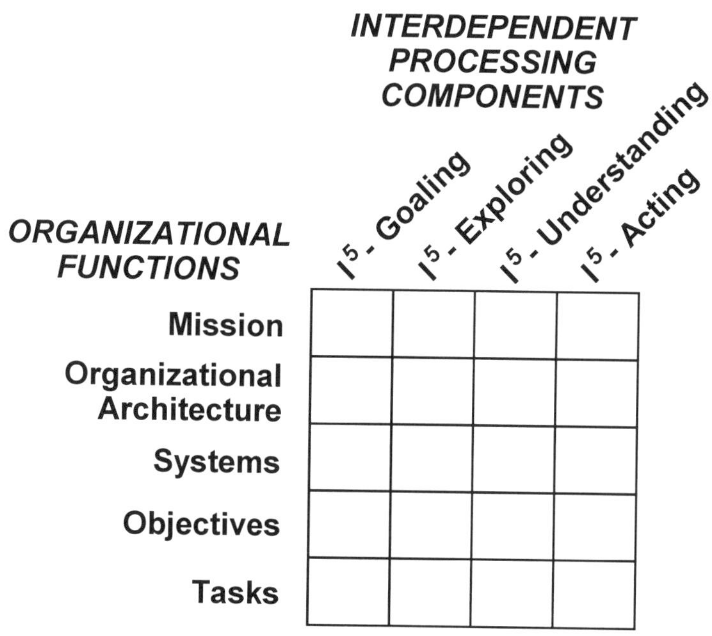

Interdependent Processing Model

To check out our own level of interdependent processing, we may append the organizational functions to our levels of interdependent processing. To qualify, we must have processed interdependently by *Get, Give, Merge and Grow* through any or all of the phases of processing: goaling, exploring, understanding, acting. These stringent requirements reflect interdependent processing as a way of life.

LEVELS OF INTERDEPENDENT PROCESSING
(Carkhuff and Berenson, 2000)

5   INTERDEPENDENT ACTING

4   INTERDEPENDENT UNDERSTANDING

3   INTERDEPENDENT EXPLORING

2   INTERDEPENDENT GOALING

1   NON-PREPARATION

Interdependent Processing Profile

We may initiate interdependent processing with the stimulus input of the merged image of HCD derived from interpersonal processing. This is our input to goaling: it is our goal to improve upon this image by processing interdependently. Accordingly, we establish our goal to *"grow"* this image of HCD.

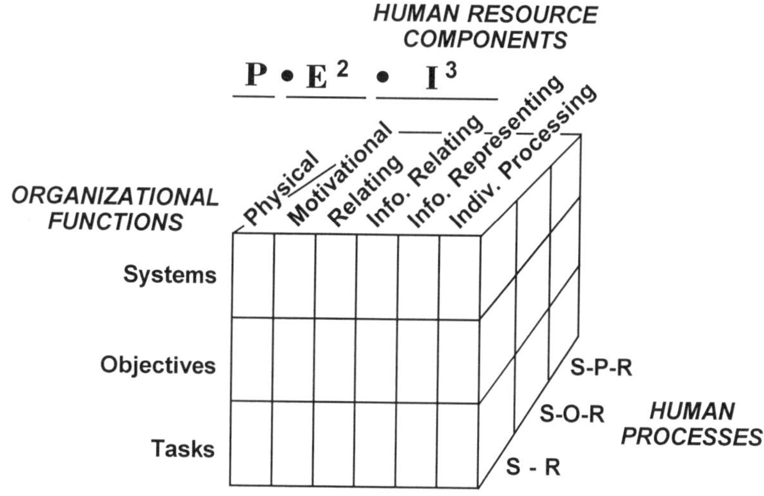

GGMG—Goaling Input

In the next phase of interdependent processing, we explore new ways of growing this image of HCD. As may be viewed below, we add organizational architecture to the organizational functions; we add interpersonal processing to the human resource components; we extend our human processes to incorporate S–OP–R generative organizational processing systems.

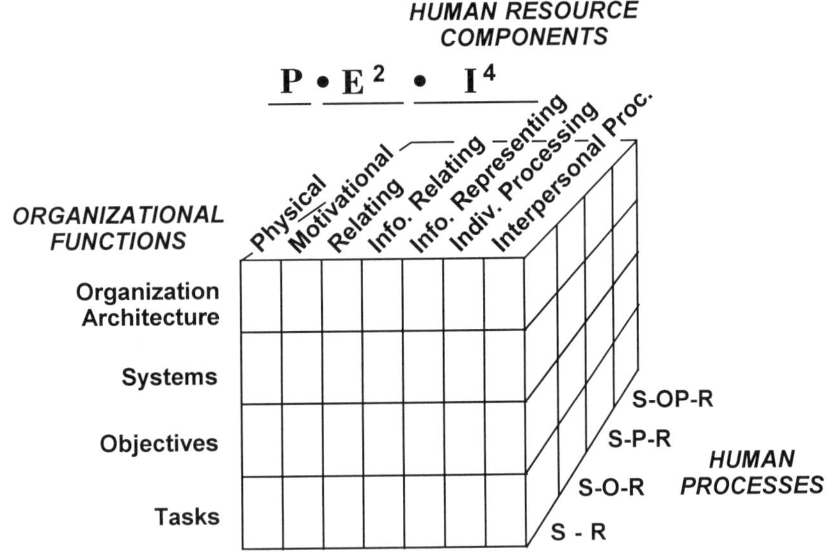

GGMG—Exploring

In the next phase of interdependent processing, understanding, we *"grow"* the image of HCD still further. As may be viewed, we add missioning to organizational functions; we add interdependent processing to human resource components; we extend our human processes to include S–PP–R phenomenal processing systems. We may now define prime HCD operationally: mission-driven functions are discharged by interdependent processing human resource components enabled by S–PP–R phenomenal processing systems.

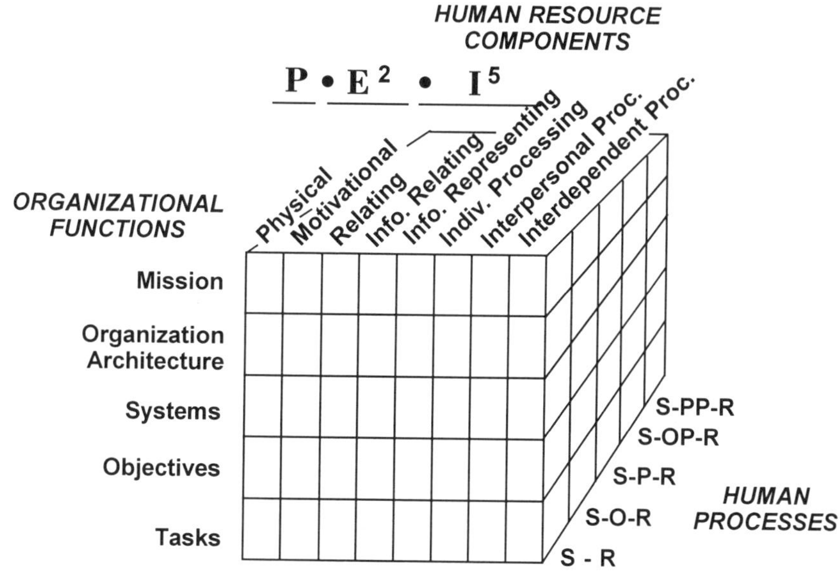

GGMG—Understanding

Finally, we may go on to plan to implement our new model for prime HCD. We define our objectives operationally and develop our steps programmatically. The foregoing was a true story of the evolution of the definition and representation of HCD through interdependent processing. We need only review our early images to understand the power of interdependent processing.

GGMG—Acting

Here, again, we may rate ourselves on our modal levels of functioning across areas. It is to be emphasized that people functioning modally at high levels are always disposed to interdependent processing. People functioning at low levels are never disposed to interdependent processing—and, thus, lose the contributions of others. We are fully actualized only if we are processing interdependently. We can only actualize our human potential with a system for interdependent processing.

Levels of Interdependent Processing	Areas of Application				
	Home	School	Work	Org.	Community
5 GGMG— Acting upon Organizations					
4 GGMG— Understanding Organizations					
3 GGMG— Exploring Organizations					
2 GGMG— Goaling Organizations					
1 Non- Preparation					

Modal Interdependent Processing Profile

We may say that we currently work with others, but do we have the skills to maximize the results of our mutual efforts? Do we currently possess the best skills to *relate*, to give and get ideas? Do we have the most well-developed skills to *elevate* ideas, synthesizing solutions beyond consensus sharing? Do we have the skills to *generate* with others, beyond our initial visions? *"Breakthroughs"* require breakthrough interdependent processes.

Interdependent Processing Skills

The growthful interdependent processor moves developmentally and cumulatively through the levels of interdependent processing. Interdependent processing culminates when people process together with phenomena to generate entirely new responses. Individual thinking and interpersonal processing are the preconditions for interdependent processing, providing individual response outputs which are then processed interdependently as stimulus inputs. If we cannot process interdependently, we cannot culminate our individual and interpersonal processing. At the highest levels, there is no interdependent processing without individual and interpersonal processing; and no individual and interpersonal processing without interdependent processing.

Interdependent Perspective

Interdependent processing is the culminating and actualizing application of human processing. Interdependent processing creates a synergistic relationship in which we generate exponentially more than the sum of the products of the independent processors. In other words, independent processing outputs become *quantitative* inputs which, in turn, are interdependently generated into *qualitative* outputs. In short, interdependent processing is the vehicle to higher-order response outputs. Ultimately, fully actualized processors think interdependently with all forms of processing phenomena—mechanical, informational, organizational and environmental as well as human. We can no longer *"grow"* independently and unilaterally. In the Age of Interdependency, we can only "grow" by interdependent processing.

The Actualizers

III

Summary and Transition

11. The HCD Operations

In my experience and testing of Americans, the modal American profile of *"Workforce XXI"* is the relatively consistent one of *"observer"* (see Table 4). Indeed, it is the very emphasis of the peer culture of the dominant *"Baby Boom"* generation to *"lay back"* and *"observe"* before a political consensus develops. Thus, the collective American profile emphasizes independent sharing rather than interdependent relating. To sum, the modal American profile is a neutral one for a people so indoctrinated historically with the competitive ethic. In short, in our homes, schools and businesses, we have produced consumers rather than processors of information.

The Model American HCD Profile

Table 4. MODAL AMERICAN HCD PROFILE

LEVELS OF FUNCTIONING	PHYSICAL	EMOTIONAL		INTELLECTUAL				
	Physical Fitness	Personal Motivation	Interpersonal Relating	Information Relating	Information Representing	Individual Processing	Interpersonal Processing	Inter-dependent Processing
Leader	Stamina	Mission	Initiate	Objectives	Multi-D	Act	Go	Interdep. Acting
Contributor	Intensity	Actualize	Personalize	Applications	Nested D	Understand	Merge	Interdep. Understand.
Participant	Adapt	Achieve	Respond	Principles	3D	Explore	Give	Interdep. Exploring
Observer	Survive	Incentive	Attend	Concepts	2D	Goal	Get	Interdep. Goaling
Detractor	Sick	Non-Incentive	Non-Attending	Facts	1D	Non-Preparation	Non-Engagement	Non-Engagement

With the exception of intellectual resources, the HCD profile may be characterized at an observer's level. There the curve attenuates: the failures of each intellectual area are the preconditions of the next area's shortcoming. All of this culminates in very shaky performances in the areas of the most formidable requirements: the intellectual area. In short, Americans do best in the areas that are no longer called for: the physical labor required during the Industrial Age. They are low in the Data Age standards required by the information technology–driven marketplace. They are poorest in meeting the requirements of the coming Information Age.

At a minimum, the American population must aspire to the participant level. Indeed, it is the independent American's emphasis upon independent contribution—without full participation—which precludes us from successfully achieving participation. It is as if our great strength has become our great weakness. Instead of building developmentally to success, Americans have become *"fixated"* in their fantasies about incentives. We would do well to aspire to become fully participative:

- Physical energy to adapt;

- Motivation to achieve;

- Interpersonal skills to respond accurately to others;

- Information relating skills to define processing operations;

- Information representing skills to model 3D operations;

- Individual processing skills to explore experience;

- Interpersonal processing skills to share images;

- Interdependent processing skills to GGMG exploring organizations.

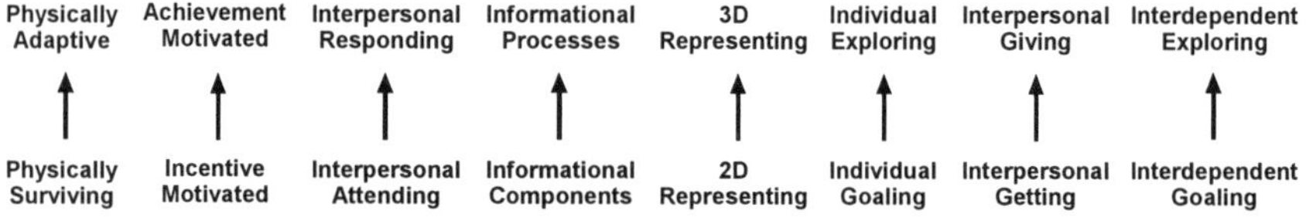

Fully Participative

To be sure, the American population has produced a spiraling array of products and services in the 20th century. But 20th century requirements for independence and competitiveness no longer suffice. The introduction of the Data Age has not yet required the extraordinary emphasis upon intellectual processing demanded by the coming Information Age. Above all else, the 21st century will be characterized by collaboration and interdependency. All of the other HCD ingredients will be developmental toward interdependent processing: I5.

I5

III. Summary and Transition

Perhaps we wish to summarize our own modal levels of functioning (see Table 5) based upon our review of the foregoing material. We may be disappointed because we have not managed to function at ideal levels. On the other hand, we may be relieved to realize that there is hope in proceeding to develop our skills, knowledge and attitudes. Most important, we must build our levels of functioning as we build our lives—developmentally and cumulatively. Hopefully, we feel eager to get going— precisely because we have reinvigorated hope!

Table 5. PERSONAL HCD PROFILE

LEVELS OF FUNCTIONING	PHYSICAL	EMOTIONAL		INTELLECTUAL			
	Physical Fitness	Personal Motivation	Interpersonal Relating	Information Relating	Information Representing	Individual Processing	Interpersonal Processing
Leader	Stamina	Mission	Initiate	Objectives	Multi-D	Act	Interdep. Acting
Contributor	Intensity	Actualize	Personalize	Applications	Nested D	Understand	Interdep. Understand.
Participant	Adapt	Achieve	Respond	Principles	3D	Explore	Interdep. Exploring
Observer	Survive	Incentive	Attend	Concepts	2D	Goal	Interdep. Goaling
Detractor	Sick	Non-Incentive	Non-Attending	Facts	1D	Non-Preparation	Non-Engagement

12. The HCD Equation

The message of this book has been simply: *it is a time to choose; it is a time to grow.* If the purpose of life is to grow, then growth is worth any price! This does not mean the end to family, business and cultural traditions. Quite the contrary, it means the enrichment of these customs. They had a survival reason for being adopted. Without the survival of our ancestors, we would not have been enabled to meet the growth choices today! We owe the greatest respect to all people and customs that made our privileged opportunities possible. To be sure, we have a responsibility to rationalize their sacrifices by our growth and fulfillment. The equation for human capital development emphasizes physical, emotional and intellectual development:

$$HCD = P \bullet E \bullet I$$

Human Growth

Let us summarize the critical dimensions of human growth. The physical dimension is the most basic dimension. Without functioning at high levels of physical energy, nothing else is possible. However, it cannot become an end in itself. Even with functioning at high levels of physical energy, nothing else is probable. In other words, physical growth is a necessary, but not sufficient, condition for everything. It is an *"enabler."* It enables but does not produce emotional or intellectual growth. It is only in interaction with these dimensions that physical energy has a contribution to make. Our physical energy level then ***"energizes"*** our emotional and intellectual functioning.

P

Human Energy

Our motivation expands the boundaries of our *intra*personal universes. Our human relations expand the boundaries of our *inter*personal universes. In interaction, each expands the boundaries of the other. Multiplied, they accelerate each other's contribution and mobilize the human emotion to grow. The motivational and interpersonal ingredients ***"catalyze"*** our intellectual functioning.

$$E^2$$

Human Emotion

In turn, the intellectual dimensions grow in synergistic relationship with one another. Information relating and representing produces input to our individual thinking which, in turn, becomes input to our interpersonal processing which, in turn, generates inputs from interdependent processing which generates *"breakthrough"* images of phenomena. Each intellectual dimension accelerates the functioning of the other dimensions. The higher the level of information relating and representing, the higher the level of individual thinking. The higher the level of thinking, the higher the level of interpersonal processing. The higher the level of interpersonal processing, the higher the level of interdependent processing. Multiplied, the intellectual dimensions become the prepotent source of human growth.

$$I^5$$

Human Intellect

To place the human capital paradigm in its most powerful perspective, we must weight the contributions of the respective factors. The intellectual dimension to the fifth power (I^5) is prepotent and overriding. Indeed, for most purposes, our intellectual functioning serves to define our growth potential and, thus, our humanity. However, it is to be emphasized that, weighted, each dimension serves to multiply the effects of the other dimensions and, thus, their value. We may conclude that the physical dimensions *"energize,"* the emotional dimensions *"catalyze,"* and the intellectual dimensions *"actualize"* our human capital development.

$$HCD = P \bullet E^2 \bullet I^5$$

HCD Potential

What lies ahead? Time is telescoped. Where humankind spent 300 years in the Industrial Age, human resources have devoted only 30 years to the Data Age. And already human capital is required! What lies ahead? A true Age of Information and, beyond that, an Age of Ideation! And each brings with it a set of elevated standards! The best of times for *"Workforce XXI!"* No time at all for less!

HCD Requirements

Most basically, humans and data will become synergistic processing partners. Indeed, data does not culminate as information capital until they are processed by human capital. Vice versa, human capital cannot be generated until it is stimulated by information capital. To be sure, the development of both of these capital sources is synergistically related: each contributes to the growth of the other. In this context, this book is my ICD contribution to your HCD!

$$HCD \leftrightarrow ICD$$

The standards emphasize increasingly higher levels of HCD:

- Physical fitness to energize our efforts;
- Motivation to catalyze our focus;
- Interpersonal skills to facilitate our relating;
- Informational relating to define information operations;
- Information representing to represent information operations;
- Individual processing to generate new images;
- Intepersonal processing to generate better images;
- Interdependent processing to actualize our contributions by generating a continuous flow of new standards.

In short, HCD skills empower us to reinvent ourselves to generate the environments in which we live and, insodoing, to generate our human destinies.

HCD

Appendices

The Evolution of
HCD Systems

Milestones in HCD

Human Relations Phase

1963   Truax and Carkhuff form *Group Therapy Research* group, Universities of Kentucky and Wisconsin, for the study of all counseling and psychotherapeutic relationships.

1964   Truax and Carkhuff's *Toward Effective Counseling and Psychotherapy* summarizes "breakthrough" research on the effective ingredients in counseling and psychotherapeutic relationships.

1965   Berenson, Carkhuff and Aspy form *HRD Research Group*, University of Massachusetts, for the study of all human relations and human resource development.

1966   Berenson and Carkhuff's *Sources of Gain in Counseling and Psychotherapy* introduces sources of HRD.

1967   Carkhuff and Berenson's *Beyond Counseling and Therapy* introduces first systematic eclectic approaches to HRD.

1968   Berenson, Carkhuff and Griffin create first *Center for HRD* at American International College, Springfield, Massachusetts.

1969   Carkhuff's *Helping and Human Relations* introduces first systematic Interpersonal Communication Skills Technologies.

1970   Creation of *Carkhuff Institute of Human Technology*, Amherst, Massachusetts, dedicated to R&D in HRD.

1971   Carkhuff's *The Development of Human Resources* introduces the effective ingredients in individual HRD.

1972   Carkhuff's *Art of Helping* introduces series presenting first systematic interpersonal, decision-making and program development technologies.

1973   Berenson's *Confrontation* introduces comprehensive research validating responsive and initiative interpersonal dimensions.

1974   Berenson creates first *Human Technology Curriculum* at American International College, Springfield, Massachusetts.

1975   Aspy and Roebuck create *National Consortium for Human Technology in Education*, Northeastern Louisiana University.

1976   Carkhuff and Berenson's *Teaching as Treatment* introduces psychological education as the preferred mode of all HRD.

1977   Carkhuff, Berenson, et al. create first systematic *Teaching and Learning Technologies.*

1978   Anthony, et al. create *Center for Research and Training in Mental Health,* for applications of psychological education, at Boston University.

1979   Carkhuff, et al. create the *Instructional System Design* and *Training Delivery Systems.*

Human Development Phase

1980   Creation of *Human Technology, Inc.,* the first private sector HT corporation dedicated to human and organizational applications.

1981   Carkhuff's *Toward Actualizing Human Potential* operationalizes HRD technologies for individual development.

1982   Carkhuff's *Interpersonal Skills and Human Productivity* summarizes two decades of HRD research involving more than 150 studies of more than 150,000 people.

1983   Carkhuff's *Sources of Human Productivity* defines first systematic technologies for organizational productivity.

1984   Carkhuff's *Exemplar* defines first systematic technologies for individual performance.

1985   Carkhuff's *Human Processing for Human Productivity* introduces first systematic individual, interpersonal and organizational processing systems.

1986   Carkhuff technologies produce first *Productive Thinking Systems.*

1987   Carkhuff technologizes first *Interdependent Processing Systems.*

1988   Carkhuff's *The Age of the New Capitalism* introduces the new capital ingredients in the equation for generating wealth.

1989   Carkhuff's *Empowering* introduces first empowering technologies for generating the new capital ingredients.

New Capital Development Phase

1990   Creation of *Carkhuff Thinking Systems, Inc.,* dedicated to the R&D of all processing systems.

1991   Berenson and Carkhuff create *The New Science of Possibilities,* generating a scientific foundation for driving *"The Science of Probabilities."*

1992   Carkhuff generates *The Monolithic Idea,* positing the integration of all processing systems, to demonstrate *"The New Science of Possibilities."*

1993   Berenson, Carkhuff and Carkhuff develop *The Unifactoral Design* to implement *The Monolithic Idea.*

1994   Carkhuff, Carkhuff, et al. define *The New Capital Development Systems* to generate new sources of wealth.

1995   Carkhuff, Carkhuff, et al. define *The Marketplace Capital Development Systems.*

1996   Carkhuff, Carkhuff, et al. define *The Organization Capital Development Systems.*

1997   Carkhuff et al. develop *The Human Capital Development Systems.*

1998   Carkhuff et al. develop *The Information Capital Development Systems.*

1999   Carkhuff publishes *Human Capital XXI—Skills for Human Capital Development in the 21st Century.*

The New Science Phase

2000   Carkhuff and Berenson publish *The New Science of Possibilities* detailing *The Processing Science* and *Processing Technologies.*

Carkhuff and Berenson develop *The New Science of Possibilities Management,* publishing *The Possibilities Leader* and *The Possibilities Organization.*

Berenson and Carkhuff publish *The Possibilities Mind— Conversations with Einstein.*

Carkhuff, Carkhuff, et al. create *Paradigmetrics* to make private sector applications of the possibilities science.

Carkhuff, Bellingham, et al. create *Possibilities, Inc.* to make public sector applications of possibilities science.

Carkhuff, et al. apply the possibilities science to education in *The New 3Rs* curriculum—Relating, Representing, Reasoning.

Carkhuff and McCune design and publish *The Possibilities Schools.*

Carkhuff, Griffin, et al. design and publish *The Possibilities Community.*

Carkhuff, Rayson, et al. design and publish *The Possibilities Economics* systems to make social economic applications and transfers of the possibilities science.

Carkhuff, Berenson, et al. design and publish *The Possibilities Culture* systems to elevate civilization through applications and transfers of a new scientific paradigm.

Bibliography

Chapter 1. The Evolution of HCD

Carkhuff, R. R. *The Development of Human Resources.* NY: Holt, Rinehart and Winston, 1971. Amherst, MA: Human Resource Development Press, 1984.

Carkhuff, R. R. *The Age of the New Capitalism.* Amherst, MA: Human Resource Development Press, 1988.

Carkhuff, R. R., and Berenson, B.G. *HCD XXI—A Blueprint for Human Capital Development.* Amherst, MA: HRD Press, 1995.

Carnavale, A. *Human Capital.* Washington, DC: ASTD, 1983.

Ginzberg, E. *Human Resources: The Wealth of a Nation.* NY: Simon and Schuster, 1958.

Chapter 2. The Ingredients of HCD

Bugelski, B. G. *Principles of Learning and Memory.* NY: Praeger, 1979.

Carkhuff, R. R. *Helping and Human Relations. Volumes 1 and 2.* NY: Holt, Rinehart and Winston, 1969. Amherst, MA: Human Resource Development Press, 1984.

Carkhuff, R. R. *The Development of Human Resources.* NY: Holt, Rinehart and Winston, 1971. Amherst, MA: Human Resource Development Press, 1984.

Carkhuff, R. R. *Toward Actualizing Human Potential.* Amherst, MA: Human Resource Development Press, 1981.

Hilgard, E., and Bower, G. *Theories of Learning.* Englewood Cliffs, NJ: Prentice-Hall, 1975.

Chapter 3. Physical Fitness—The Energizers

Bellingham, R., and Cohen, B. *The Corporate Wellness Sourcebook.* Amherst, MA: Human Resource Development Press, 1987.

Carkhuff, R. R. *Toward Actualizing Human Potential.* Amherst, MA: Human Resource Development Press, 1981.

Collingwood, T. R. *Physical Fitness—Skills Training.* Dallas, TX: Institute for Aerobics Research, 1992.

Collingwood, T., and Carkhuff, R. R. *Get Fit for Living.* Amherst, MA: Human Resource Development Press, 1974.

Cooper, K. *Aerobics.* Dallas, TX: Aerobics Center, 1972.

Chapter 4. Personal Motivation—The Catalyzers

Carkhuff, R. R. *Toward Actualizing Human Potential.* Amherst, MA: Human Resource Development Press, 1981.

Carkhuff, R. R. *Sources of Human Productivity.* Amherst, MA: Human Resource Development Press, 1983.

Herzberg, F. *Work and the Nature of Man.* NY: World Publishing, 1966.

Maslow, A. H. *Motivation and Personality.* NY: Harper and Row, 1954.

McLelland, D. *The Achieving Society.* NY: Van Nostrand Reinhold, 1961.

Chapter 5. Interpersonal Relating—The Facilitators

Carkhuff, R. R. *Helping and Human Relations. Volumes 1 and 2.* NY: Holt, Rinehart and Winston, 1969. Amherst, MA: Human Resource Development Press, 1984.

Carkhuff, R. R. *The Development of Human Resources.* NY: Holt, Rinehart and Winston, 1971. Amherst, MA: Human Resource Development Press, 1984.

Carkhuff, R. R. *The Art of Helping.* Amherst, MA: Human Resource Development Press, 1984.

Carkhuff, R. R. *Interpersonal Skills and Human Productivity.* Amherst, MA: Human Resource Development Press, 1983.

Carkhuff, R. R., and Berenson, B. G. *Beyond Counseling and Psychotherapy.* Amherst, MA: Human Resource Development Press, 1967.

Chapter 6. Information Relating—The Operationalizers

Bloom, B. S., Englehart, M. D., Furst, E. J., Hill, W. H., and Krathwohl, D. R. *A Taxonomy of Educational Objectives. Handbook I: The Cognitive Domain.* NY: Longmans, Green, 1956.

Carkhuff, R. R. *Learning and Thinking in the Age of Information.* McLean, VA: Carkhuff Institute of Human Technology, 1988.

Carkhuff, R. R., et al. *The Skills of Teaching. Volumes 1–4.* Amherst, MA: Human Resource Development Press, 1977–1981.

Carkhuff, R. R., et al. *Instructional Systems Design.* Amherst, MA: Human Resource Development Press, 1983.

Mager, R. R. *Preparing Instructional Objectives.* Palo Alto, CA: Fearon Publishing, 1972.

Chapter 7. Information Representing—The Modelers

Carkhuff, R. R., and Berenson, B. G. *The Possibilities Leader.* Amherst, MA: HRD Press, 2000.
Carkhuff, R. R., and Berenson, B. G. *The Possibilities Organization.* Amherst, MA: HRD Press, 2000.
Gilbert, T. F. *Human Competence.* NY: McGraw-Hill, 1978.
Mager R. F. *Preparing Objectives for Programmed Instruction.* San Francisco: Fearon Publishers, 1962.
Taylor, F. W. *Principles of Scientific Management.* NY: W.W. Norton, 1967.

Chapter 8. Individual Processing—The Thinkers

Carkhuff, R. R. *Human Processing and Human Productivity.* Amherst, MA: Human Resource Development Press, 1986.

Carkhuff, R. R. *Learning and Thinking in the Age of Information.* McLean, VA: Carkhuff Institute of Human Technology, 1988.

Carkhuff, R. R. *Productive Thinking Systems.* McLean, VA: Carkhuff Thinking Systems, 1991.

Hull, C. L. *Essentials of Behavior*. New Haven: Yale University Press, 1951.

Skinner, B. F. *The Behavior of Organisms*. NY: Appleton-Century-Crofts, 1938.

Chapter 9. Interpersonal Processing—The Shared Processors

Carkhuff, R. R. *Sources of Human Productivity*. Amherst, MA: Human Resource Development Press, 1983.

Carkhuff, R. R. *The Exemplar—The Exemplary Performer in the Age of Information*. Amherst, MA: Human Resource Development Press, 1984.

Carkhuff, R. R. *Human Processing and Human Productivity*. Amherst, MA: Human Resource Development Press, 1986.

Carkhuff, R. R. *Learning and Thinking in the Age of Information*. McLean, VA: Carkhuff Institute of Human Technology, 1988.

Carkhuff, R. R. *Empowering*. Amherst, MA: Human Resource Development Press, 1989.

Chapter 10. Interdependent Processing— The Actualizers

Berenson, B. G., and Carkhuff, R. R. *The Possibilities Mind*. Amherst, MA: HRD Press, 2000.

Carkhuff, R. R., and Berenson, B. G. *The New Science of Possibilities I. The Processing Science*. Amherst, MA: HRD Press, 2000.

Carkhuff, R. R., and Berenson, B. G. *The New Science of Possibilities II. The Processing Technologies*. Amherst, MA: HRD Press, 2000.

Carkhuff, R. R., and Berenson, B. G. *The Possibilities Leader*. Amherst, MA: HRD Press, 2000.

Carkhuff, R. R., and Berenson, B. G. *The Possibilities Organizations*. Amherst, MA: HRD Press, 2000.

Chapter 11. The HCD Operations

Carkhuff, R. R. *Sources of Human Productivity*. Amherst, MA: Human Resource Development Press, 1983.
Carkhuff, R. R. *Toward Actualizing Human Potential*. Amherst, MA: Human Resource Development Press, 1981.
Carkhuff, R. R. *The Exemplar—The Exemplary Performer in the Age of Information*. Amherst, MA: Human Resource Development Press, 1984.
Carkhuff, R. R. *Human Processing and Human Productivity*. Amherst, MA: Human Resource Development Press, 1986.
Carkhuff, R. R., and Berenson, B. G. *The Possibilities Leader*. Amherst, MA: HRD Press, 2000.

Chapter 12. The HCD Equation

Berenson, B. G., and Carkhuff, R. R. *The Possibilities Mind*. Amherst, MA: HRD Press, 2000.

Carkhuff, R. R. *The Age of the New Capitalism*. Amherst, MA: HRD Press, 1988.

Carkhuff, R. R. *Empowering*. Amherst, MA: HRD Press, 1989.

Carkhuff, R. R., and Berenson, B. G. *The New Science of Possibilities. Volumes I & II*. Amherst, MA: HRD Press, 2000.

ACKNOWLEDGMENTS

First, I would like to acknowledge the contributions of the core of research associates in Carkhuff Thinking Systems, Inc., who helped to develop some of the ideas presented in this work:

- Don Benoit, M.A., who contributed operations to information representation
- Chris Carkhuff, M.A. Cert., who developed the organizational capital models
- Alvin Cook, Ph.D., who built math models and coding systems
- Barbara Emmert, Ph.D., who provided an information systems perspective
- Dave Meyers, M.A., who engineered organizational applications

In addition, I owe a special debt to a number of people—themselves *"possibilities managers"* who made applications of my work at Human Technology, Inc.:

- John Cannon, Ph.D., Vice President, New Capital Development
- Alex Douds, M.A., Director, Performance Systems Group
- Sharon Fisher, M.A., Chief Operating Officer
- Ted W. Friel, Ph.D., Information Technology Consultant
- Richard Pierce, Ph.D., Director, Organizational Consulting Group

I am particularly indebted to those scientists who contributed early on to my overall thinking:

- David N. Aspy, D.Ed., Carkhuff Institute
- George Banks, D.Ed., Carkhuff Institute
- David H. Berenson, Ph.D., Carkhuff Institute
- Ralph Bierman, Ph.D., Carkhuff Institute

- B. R. Bugelski, Ph.D., S.U.N.Y. at Buffalo
- James Drasgow, Ph.D., S.U.N.Y. at Buffalo
- Gerald Oliver, M.S., Carkhuff Institute
- Flora N. Roebuck, D.Ed., Carkhuff Institute
- Richard Sprinthall, Ph.D., American International College

I also owe gratitude to pathfinders in business and industry who gave me opportunities to make applications:

- Rick Bellingham, Ph.D., Gensyme, Inc.
- Russ Campanello, Genzyme, Inc.
- Dave Champaign, Lotus Corp., IBM
- Barry Cohen, Ph.D., Parametric Technology Corp.
- John T. Kelly, M.A., IBM
- Bill O'Brien, M.A., Parametric Technology Corp.
- Russ Planitzer, Lazard, Inc.
- Jack Riley, IBM
- Peter Rayson, M.Sc., C. Eng., Parametric Technology Corp.
- Carl Turner, General Electric
- Norman Turner, General Electric

I am also indebted to educational advisors with whom I processed interdependently to make extensive applications:

- William Anthony, Ph.D., Boston University
- Sally Berenson, D.Ed., North Carolina State University
- Karen Banks, D.Ed., James Madison University
- Terry Bergeson, D.Ed., Superintendent of Public Instruction, Washington
- Mikal Cohen, Ph.D., Boston University
- Andrew H. Griffin, D.Ed., Assistant Superintendent of Public Instruction, Washington
- Shirley McCune, Ph.D., Assistant Superintendent of Public Instruction, Washington
- Jeannette Tamagini, Ph.D., Rhode Island College

Also, I express my gratitude to the trainers of Human Capital Development at the HRD Center, American International College, for piloting some of my work:

- Debbie Decker Anderson, D.Ed., Director
- Cindy Littlefield, M.A., Associate Director
- Susan Mackler, M.A., Holyoke Community College
- Richard Muise, M.A., Assistant Director

There are those who deserve my appreciation for their support in transforming these early manuscripts into readable books:

- Dave Burleigh, D B Associates, for marketing
- Bob Carkhuff, Jr., HRD Press, for positioning
- John Cannon, Ph.D., Human Technology, Inc., for his critical readings
- Mary George, M.A., HRD Press, for editing

Jean Miller deserves an exceptional note of recognition for implementing my *"rapid prototyping"* method of writing: about one dozen versions of each book were produced before final copy. Not only did she turn around high-quality typing, she also turned around high quality with timeliness. Not only did she generate creative graphics and layout, she also continuously retrieved lost files and, on at least two occasions, tracked down misdelivered manuscripts. These books are as much her books as mine!

Finally, I owe a debt of everlasting love and gratitude to the person who has been absolute in her commitment to enabling me to actualize my vision: my wife, Bernice, who related to my experience, empowered my potential, and released me to the freedom of my scientific pursuits. For nearly 50 years, I have been saying, *"Give me another year and I'll get there."* Well, the *year* is up! And I got there!